WHO DO YOU WANT TO BE
WHEN YOU GROW OLD?

WHO DO YOU WANT TO BE WHEN YOU GROW OLD?

The Path of Purposeful Aging

RICHARD J. LEIDER
DAVID A. SHAPIRO

BK

Berrett–Koehler Publishers, Inc.

Berrett-Koehler Publishers, Inc.
1333 Broadway, Suite 1000
Oakland, CA 94612-1921
Tel: (510) 817-2277
Fax: (510) 817-2278
www.bkconnection.com

ORDERING INFORMATION
Quantity sales. Special discounts are available on quantity purchases by corporations, associations, and others. For details, contact the "Special Sales Department" at the Berrett-Koehler address above.

Individual sales. Berrett-Koehler publications are available through most bookstores. They can also be ordered directly from Berrett-Koehler: Tel: (800) 929-2929; Fax: (802) 864-7626; www.bkconnection.com.

Orders for college textbook/course adoption use. Please contact Berrett-Koehler:
Tel: (800) 929-2929; Fax: (802) 864-7626.

Distributed to the U.S. trade and internationally by Penguin Random House Publisher Services.

Berrett-Koehler and the BK logo are registered trademarks of Berrett-Koehler Publishers, Inc.

Printed in the United States of America

Berrett-Koehler books are printed on long-lasting acid-free paper. When it is available, we choose paper that has been manufactured by environmentally responsible processes. These may include using trees grown in sustainable forests, incorporating recycled paper, minimizing chlorine in bleaching, or recycling the energy produced at the paper mill.

Library of Congress Cataloging-in-Publication Data

Names: Leider, Richard, author. | Shapiro, David, 1947– author.
Title: Who do you want to be when you grow old? : the path of purposeful aging / Richard J. Leider, David A. Shapiro.
Description: 1st Edition. | Oakland : Berrett-Koehler Publishers, 2021. | Includes index.
Identifiers: LCCN 2021008110 | ISBN 9781523092451 (hardcover) | ISBN 9781523092468 (adobe pdf) | ISBN 9781523092475 (epub)
Subjects: LCSH: Older people—Psychology. | Older people—Conduct of life. | Self-realization.
Classification: LCC BF724.8 .L45 2021 | DDC 155.67—dc23
LC record available at https://lccn.loc.gov/2021008110

First Edition

27 26 25 24 23 22 21   10 9 8 7 6 5 4 3 2 1

Book production: Linda Jupiter Productions   *Edit:* Elissa Rabellino
Text design: Kim Scott, Bumpy Design   *Proofread:* Maty Kanable
Cover design: Wes Youssi, M.80 Design   Index: Paula C. Durbin-Westby

To everyone, everywhere,
who is growing older

Contents

....

Choosing the Path

This is a book by two old friends who have known each other more than half of both their lives. It is a book that explores a subject about which no one can claim absolute expertise, but which each of us learns a little bit more about every day. It is a book whose purpose is purpose.

It is a book about how to grow old, with the emphasis on "grow." Our focus is not just on getting older but also on how to grow as we do so. Everyone is getting older; not everyone is growing older. This is a book about growing whole as we grow old and how the later years of our lives can be as fulfilling and meaningful as those that led us here—if not more so. We see aging as a liberating experience, one that enables us to live with greater purpose and meaning for all of our lives.

Our pairing of backgrounds in psychology and philosophy and our nearly 150 years of growing older give us, as coauthors and friends, a unique perspective on the path of purposeful aging. The questions we raise are open to reflection by everyone, and the answers that arise in response are for each of us to consider personally as they relate to our own lives.

We grow up twice: first, from childhood to adulthood; second, from adulthood to elderhood.

We grow up twice: first, from childhood to adulthood; second, from adulthood to elderhood. Taking the path of purposeful aging means outgrowing adulthood and growing into elderhood, expressing more of our true selves in all that we do. Purpose and meaning emerge from choosing to follow our own path. The path is marked by a mindset that the second half of life—the "old" half—is less about outward accomplishment and more about inward growth.

The path of purposeful aging is a choice to wake up every day with the intention to grow and give. Choice is the key. Later life affords us the freedom to choose to become the person we always meant to be. Too many of us live the first half of our lives by default; the choices we made were typically made for us by societal expectations, custom, and external demands. In later life, no longer constrained by those default choices, we are finally free to choose to become the person we really are, the most complete and authentic expression of our deepest self.

Purpose is our *why*—why to get up in the morning. It's the path that gives our life meaning. All of us are on that path, just at different

Purpose is our why—*why to get up in the morning.*

places along it, at different stages in our lives. Everyone is getting older; not everyone is growing older.

The path of purposeful aging is to be traveled for three reasons. First, it is energizing and life-affirming; it provides us with that *why* to get up in the morning. Second, it makes us more resilient as we face the inevitable adversities of aging. And third, it enables us to grow whole as we grow older.

We, Richard Leider and Dave Shapiro, have long traveled our paths together as friends, colleagues, and coauthors. We met back in the 20th century, when Richard was still known as Dick Leider and Dave made sure to be called David A. Shapiro. The name change for Richard happened soon after the publication of our first book, *Repacking Your Bags: Lighten Your Load for the Good Life*, when he approached the half-century mark and began taking himself more seriously as a writer and speaker. And coincidentally, when Dave turned 50, about the time our third book, *Claiming Your Place at the Fire: Living the Second Half of Your Life on Purpose*, came out and he started taking himself on the whole less seriously, he began introducing himself with the shortened moniker.

This is simply to illustrate in one small way our abiding belief that growth can continue to happen from cradle to grave. The path of purposeful aging is always open to us if we're willing to keep growing; it will be different for everyone but is accessible to all.

When we were children, grown-ups often asked, "What do you want to be when you grow up?" The answers we gave were typically ones that Dave still hears from second-graders when he leads Philosophy for Children classes with them: doctor, basketball player, veterinarian, teacher. (Although nowadays, some seven-year-olds answer that when they grow up, they want to be video game designers or YouTube creators, professions unheard-of in our youth.)

It's the *what* that children emphasize: an occupation or profession. Some *what* that will fulfill their dreams of a good life. All fine and perfectly understandable, of course.

When we become adults, though, and have lived that *what*, a new and different—but related—question emerges, one we ask *ourselves*: "*Who* do I want to be when I grow old?" The shift from *what* to *who* is key here. In our later years, many of us will find the *what* by which we defined ourselves falling away. Whether or not we can or will retire, it is inevitable that this formal—typically vocational—structure of our lives—the *what*—will become less important. What we do will turn out to be secondary to *who* we are. The person we've always been, or been so far, often emerges more authentically.

The question is: Will that emergent creature be like a butterfly casting off its cocoon and ready to spread its wings for the next phase of life or more like the proverbial deer in the headlights, paralyzed with fear?

Or, to put it more directly: How can we *grow* old rather than merely *get* old as we age?

What's next? What are my real possibilities in life at this age? are questions most of us will ask ourselves sooner or later. If we're able to reimagine our lives and our sense of purpose, then we can look forward to a more fulfilling, meaningful life at any age. The path of purposeful aging is a process of reimagination.

> *The path of purposeful aging is a process of reimagination.*

Some people live their adult lives repeating the same year over and over without ever rocking the boat. Others choose to live their lives as an adventure of possibility and growth. As we age, we can choose to reimagine our lives in a manner that enables us to live in new and more fulfilling ways.

Most of us will live longer than past generations. Yet the societal story of aging is stuck in a script from our grandparents' or great-grandparents' era. As such, it's not doing us any favors.

The time has come to change that story from a default antiaging mindset to an intentional pro-aging mindset. It's time to retire retirement as we know it.

We must stop viewing aging as a disease. Aging is not a disease; it is a design problem. Growing old is not a bug in life's program; it is a feature. Reimagining our lives for longer lives requires that we choose to grow whole, not just old. And that means exploring the path of purposeful aging.

We have chosen our subtitle, "The Path of Purposeful Aging," to emphasize that aging on purpose is a journey rather than a destination. It's a quest, of sorts, to experience the power of purpose in later life, within a culture that tends to see old age as something to be feared. The quest is marked by *questions* that allow us to look back on our lives in order to grow and to look forward toward the future in order to give. That theme, "to grow and to give," is a universal expression of purpose in later life, one that each of us can adapt and adopt for our own experience.

We invite you to explore this path of purposeful aging, keeping in mind that for each of us, the path will be unique. Each of us is an experiment of one.

The path of purposeful aging is age-agnostic. It embodies principles and practices that anyone of any age can embrace. A person can (and should) start growing old well before they start getting old. Living longer requires taking the long view.

Choosing one's own path of purposeful aging is not a luxury. It is fundamental to well-being, throughout the course of one's life. It's not a goal to finally be enjoyed when one reaches "a certain age." The purposeful-aging path and practices have a powerful effect on health, healing, happiness, and, ultimately, longevity.

What is purpose? Purpose is our aim to live a life that is meaningful and makes a positive contribution to the world. It is grounded in the truth that our lives are fundamentally worth living and that

> *Purpose is our aim to live a life that is meaningful and makes a positive contribution to the world.*

each of us matters. It helps us to make sense of our lives and to organize our choices and direction in life. Purpose is dynamic; it will naturally change over the course of a lifetime. The power of purpose grows as we grow.

We don't find our purpose, because it's not something we have to go out and look for; rather, it's something we unlock by going inside—by getting to know what we stand for, what we won't stand for, and who stands with us.

Purpose always involves something that we love to do and enjoy sharing with others, that we feel passionate and care deeply about, and that we feel fits our values and the way we prefer to live and work in the world. Our purpose will always express our true gifts, passions, and values for the sake of others—no exceptions.

The path of purposeful aging involves a growth mindset in which we wake up every day with the attitude that we can continue growing and giving in spite of the adversities of aging. Purposeful aging is about looking inside and awakening to new possibilities.

It's about asking questions—questions that enable us to look within, to review our past and grow from it, and to reimagine our future, at any age. Questions like these:

+ Old? Who, me?

+ If we all end up dying, what's the purpose of living?

+ Aren't I somebody?

+ Am I living the good life my whole life?

+ How do I stop living a default life?

+ Am I having a late-life crisis?

+ Will I earn a passing grade in life?

+ How can I grow whole as I grow old?

+ How will my music play on?

As we explore these questions, we do not pretend to have all the answers, but having been on the path of purposeful aging for a long time together, we offer our insights informed by these explorations.

This is the path we're committed to follow as we grow old; we hope you'll travel your own path together with us.

WHO DO YOU WANT TO BE
WHEN YOU GROW OLD?

Introduction

....

The Long Conversation

Books like this often begin with a signature story that illustrates or frames the author's central message. We followed that convention in each of our previous works.

For example, our first book, *Repacking Your Bags*, opens with a story Richard tells about trekking across the Serengeti Plain in East Africa, wherein his guide, a Maasai tribesman named Koyie, becomes intrigued and puzzled about all the gear Richard has brought on their safari. This gives rise to Koyie's question, "Does all this make you happy?" which inspires a broader inquiry about all we are carrying as we journey through life and ultimately results in the central concept in *Repacking*: to lighten our load in order to live the good life, which we define as "Living in the place you belong, with people you love, doing the right work, on purpose."

Our story this time around, by contrast, is hardly a story at all. In fact, it's more of a conversation—a long conversation. And its locale could scarcely be less exotic: Minneapolis, Minnesota, Target Field, the home of the Twin Cities' professional baseball team, the Twins.

And the event around which it centers is actually a nonevent: a rained-out baseball game. What's relevant, though, is that something that *didn't happen* turns out to be an occasion for something to happen. As with growing old, absence leads to presence. What may have seemed empty fills in with possibility.

It's like what happens as we age: having less that we're required *to do* means we have more freedom to choose *to be.* Having fewer outward responsibilities allows for greater inward growth. We're playing a different game in later life, one in which the game itself becomes secondary and what really matters are the relationships among the players and the choices we make about how to play on purpose.

> *Having fewer outward responsibilities allows for greater inward growth.*

In this case, the absence of a baseball game led to a long conversation, communication from the heart, without holding back, revealing our true selves—*real conversation* that deepened our understanding of ourselves, of each other, of our longtime friendship, and of how, contrary to one of the dominant messages of our culture, older can be better.

It became obvious that what mattered was not the play on the field but rather the interplay between us. It wasn't about the game; it was about the unfolding conversation.

With each passing year of friendship, the conversation becomes more authentic, courageous, and meaningful. Growing old is about savoring our relationship, deepening it, and becoming more transparent in speaking our truth.

In a sense, this allows us to play the game even without the game, as this story, undramatic as it may be, is intended to illustrate.

In the summer of 2018, we had spent a couple of days together at the Leider household on the St. Croix River, about an hour from Minneapolis, catching up with each other as we have done every few years over the years and brainstorming about what our next project together might be—discussions that eventually led to this book. Having worked hard for 48 hours, and as a way to connect over a shared experience at the end of our time together, before Dave was to fly back that evening to Seattle, we were treating ourselves to a Twins game. Richard had used his connections in and around the Twin Cities to get us some fantastic seats—front row, field level, right by third base. We arrived at the park a good half-hour before the first pitch, got ourselves some refreshments, and settled into our seats, ready to enjoy the game.

But things didn't go as planned. As soon as the starting pitchers finished their pregame warm-ups, it began to rain; tarps were brought out to cover the field. The public-address announcer informed the crowd there would be a delay. We looked at each other, shrugged, and figured, what the heck—Midwest weather in the summer; just wait 20 minutes and it will change.

So, we rose from our seats and began to take a walk, under cover, around the stadium's concourse. There was an exhibit, among the other historical exhibits, about the Twins' World Series victory in 1987, some 30 years before. It reminded us that we had known each other for even longer than that.

We met in 1986, when Richard came to lead a workshop at a company in Santa Fe, New Mexico, where Dave was working at the time. Our old joke is that the content of Richard's workshop, finding your purpose, was supposed to help employees link their purpose to the company's mission so they could commit to it and foster greater organization success. Thanks to Richard's influence, however, Dave discovered that his purpose was elsewhere, and within a few months he and his wife had decamped from Santa Fe to France, where Dave pursued his dream of being an expatriate writer in Paris.

While in Europe, and subsequently—as his aspirations to be the next F. Scott Fitzgerald didn't quite pan out and he returned to the States to pursue more traditional forms of employment—Dave stayed in touch with Richard, mainly through that old-fashioned form of communication, the postal letter. This led him to Minnesota, where, among other things, he and Richard developed a closer connection, a connection that eventually resulted in our collaboration, as cowriters, on *Repacking Your Bags*.

Our reminiscences, like the rain at Target Field, continued. We strolled into an underground snack bar, packed with slightly soggy baseball fans, for some chips and another beer as we reflected on our long friendship and carried on the real conversation about purpose and meaning in life that we had been having for years, but never with such transparency and candor.

In the years that followed, as Dave pursued a graduate degree in philosophy and later became a tenured faculty member at a Seattle-area college, and as Richard's acclaim as a pioneer in the purpose movement grew, our conversation deepened. We wrote several more books together; Richard married Sally, and Dave and his wife, Jennifer, were honored guests at the occasion. Dave and Jen had a daughter, now a young adult; Richard's children grew up, and he and Sally became grandparents. Life, as they say, has gone on.

Likewise, the rain at Target Field went on. We continued to look back on the years we had known each other. As with many longtime friendships, there were fallow periods, when we would go months with little or no communication. Nevertheless, our connection ran deep.

As with baseball, our friendship has had some hits, like our collaboration on *Repacking Your Bags*, whose success exceeded our wildest expectations and provided the motivation for subsequent works together. There have been, also as in baseball, long stretches when very little happens, but also times of great activity, like when we worked on this book and talked or emailed nearly every day. We've supported each other through the loss of parents, friends, and other loved ones, and through health challenges—our own and our spouses—and we've also celebrated successes: Dave's fulfilling a lifelong dream of teaching philosophy to children in India; Richard's leading three decades of Inventure Safaris in Tanzania, East Africa.

We are *old* friends: we are both old now, and our friendship is older; and yet, through long conversation, it is continually renewed.

What we noticed, though, watching the rain come down, soaking the infield and outfield, is that when our culture conceives of something old like a friendship, the older it is, in most cases, the better. Like fine wine, it improves with age. It becomes more valuable, more honored. An *old friendship* like ours is seen as something special, beautiful, to be treasured.

By contrast, the dominant societal narrative about the old friends themselves is not so positive. By and large, old people are often portrayed by contemporary society as less than, as in the way, as a drain on society. Getting old is a condition to be avoided at all costs.

So, as we began to formulate our ideas for this book, we explored ways to overcome that gap between old as valuable and old as problematic. And, somewhat to our surprise, the rainout at Target Field (the game was eventually called) provided a metaphor for us to draw upon.

In a rainout, the event you expect to happen never happens. The one thing you're waiting for—the game—never takes place. But at the same time, everything happens. Life, and especially the opportunity to connect and converse, presents itself ever more clearly.

Aging is much like that. For most of us, the "game" changes; action on the field plays less of a role in our day-to-day living. Now, it's more of an inward game. We have the time to be more reflective and contemplative about how we want to play that game for the rest of our lives.

As such, we have a greater freedom than ever before to finally become the person we've always felt we were meant to be. That is the singular promise of growing old—that we will experience a freedom in our lives we've never before fully experienced.

> *That is the singular promise of growing old— that we will experience a freedom in our lives we've never before fully experienced.*

Above all, it's about unlocking a sense of purpose and growing old in accordance with it.

Richard has identified his own path to growing whole in simple terms: "To grow and to give." Growing and giving provides a structure for looking forward toward what Parker Palmer has called "on the brink of everything" in his 2018 book by the same name, a model that helps us face our mortality as a way to embrace life in our later years.

To grow and to give—now Richard's stated purpose —has informed the overall structure of this book. Throughout, we look back over lessons learned in the first half of life in order to grow whole. We wonder together about what we wanted to be when we grew up and how that played out. We explore what it means to be *somebody* and how becoming older has informed our view of what it means to live a good life for our whole lives.

The questions we ask each other, and the answers we explore together, have given us the chapter titles and framed the content for each one. There are nine of them, like the nine innings of the game that didn't happen. The game may have been rained out, but we share with you this opportunity to have a real conversation on purpose.

Our day together at Target Field was not what we originally had in mind for it. As with life, it didn't turn out the way we had planned, but also like life, it afforded us the opportunity to grow more whole together. What didn't happen—the ballgame—led to what did happen—a long conversation—and through the unfolding of this conversation, we are able give you this book from our hearts, on purpose.

Chapter One

Old? Who, Me?

The old joke about there being two types of people in the world—those who divide the world into two types and those who don't—reminds us that, to some extent, all distinctions are arbitrary. That being said, most of us would agree that our lives do fall into two distinct halves—a morning and an evening.

A more honest, if less poetic, way of putting it would be to admit that for half of our life we're young and for half of our life we're not. Let's be frank: there's the young half of our life and there's the old half.

Our culture is a young-half-of-life culture. The focus is on the external dimension of life: developing our outward-focused plans and goals, looking after our relationships and our livelihoods. It's about ascent. Success is often measured externally, by such criteria as how much money we make or the quality of our creative efforts or our social status.

The old half of life gets a bad rap; it's seen as largely about descent: declining health, financial insecurity, a downward spiral that's more or less inevitable.

In this book, and in our lives and work, we reject that narrative. Both halves of life are equally important and equally worthwhile. After all, if they weren't equal, they wouldn't be halves, right?

Success, in the old half of life, is measured internally, not externally. So, it's harder to see. When we're old, success is about growing our inner life rather than our outward success. When we're growing inwardly, we're succeeding.

Sometimes we're pushed by pain; other times we're pulled by possibilities. Purposeful aging requires letting go of previously held assumptions about aging. Often, it requires being impelled by a crisis of some sort—a life crucible—to move us inward. The structure of the first half of life has to fall apart to some degree and show itself to be wanting, or we will not be motivated to grow.

> *Admitting "I am old" does not mean that we accept decline; rather it means we recognize that we've moved into the half of our life that's beyond external achievement.*

Admitting "I am old" does not mean that we accept decline; rather it means we recognize that we've moved into the half of our life that's beyond external achievement. It's not about slowly dying; it's about staying alive in ways that allow us to express who we truly are more fully.

In the old half of life, we discover that it's no longer fulfilling to find meaning in simply being outwardly successful or physically appealing. We need a new story, a new language, and new models of what it means to be old.

What's in a Name?

We have chosen to use the word *old* to describe ourselves, emphasizing the idea of *growing old* rather than merely *getting old*. We freely admit that we enjoy being old and that we embrace (most of) the experiences associated with our advancing years.

The way we see it, there is a certain sense of power and agency in claiming the word *old* for ourselves. It's analogous to the way in which marginalized groups have taken ownership of terms that were historically used to describe them in a derogatory way, such as the LGBTQ community pridefully adopting the word *queer* to self-identify.

Thus, "We're old," we say, "and proud of it!"

We realize, however, that not everyone feels the way we do. For many people, the word *old* remains negative. "Old? Who, me?" they say. "Old is a state of mind; you're only as old as you feel, and I feel younger than ever!" This antiaging mindset is pervasive.

Point being: the word itself doesn't matter as much as the mindset behind it—a mindset emphasizing the

pro-aging conviction that later life is about real possibilities. Consequently, we believe you should adopt
the term to describe your age that best suits you and
best describes the age and stage you perceive yourself
to be.

Some of the terms we've heard include *elder, well-der,
older adult, oldish, person of a certain age, aged, aging person, senior citizen, retiree, sage, gray, coot, perennial, geezer*
(Dave's favorite), and *fossil* (which always brings a smile
to Richard's face). In short, if age is just a number, then
old is just a word, one of many to choose from. So, pick
the term that works best for you—or employ more than
one, as we do from time to time in our writing.

After a certain age, we're surely old enough to do so.

How Old Is "Old"?

Why do some people "of a certain age" identify as old,
while others don't? How old is "old," anyway? And if old is
a mindset, can we be old on our own terms?

Dave was 28 when he met Richard, who was 41 at that
time—not old, but certainly, to Dave's 20-something
eyes, grown up. He owned a house and had kids—both
signs, to a young person's mind, of moving one foot
toward (if not into) the grave.

There was a guy Dave worked with, though, who he
considered legitimately old. Doug was 53—a geezer, if
you asked the 28-year-old: used-up, out of touch, ancient.
He was just so slow, and serious, and kind of fragile;

never once did he go out drinking and dancing with Dave and his friends on Monday nights!

Now, however, from the perspective of a 63-year-old, 53 doesn't seem old at all; it's middle-aged at most. People who are 53 have yet to earn their first senior discount; they probably haven't even started opening their mailings from AARP.

Today, Dave's former coworker would be 88. Is that old? Chronologically, perhaps, but it depends on the person. When Richard is 88, he might be old, but maybe not. So, maybe old *is* just a mindset. The seven- and eight-year-old students that Dave teaches consider the college students he brings to their class to be old, and their perspective on his age is one of complete mystery. When he asks them how old they think he is, their eyes get wide: "Eighty?" one asks. "Ninety?" guesses another. When he admits that he is 63, one kid says, "Wow! You don't look a day older than 62!" To them, Dave is old, impossibly so, especially when he points out that when they're his age, it will be 2076.

With this in mind, the term *old* is subjective; it depends on the perspective of the person using it.

College students are old to the second-graders, but they're not really old. On the other hand, the term *old* does have an objective dimension. Dave's former coworker, at 88, probably qualifies as objectively old—but maybe not, depending on the person. As for someone aged 63, it might depend on the person's characteristics and attitude. And Richard, at 76? He's young at heart, and vital, and curious, and healthy, but does that mean he's not old?

The real issue is the way in which the word *old* is used: not as a descriptive term but as a value judgment. Calling someone (especially oneself) "old" can be an insult; to be old means used up, washed up, and basically irrelevant.

In this light, identifying a person as "old" pigeonholes them. It limits their possibilities and constrains their options. All of a sudden, someone is *too old* for something and of too little interest to someone else.

Small wonder, therefore, that so many older people find themselves trapped in a cruel paradox: they aspire to active aging but simultaneously dread the prospect of getting older. Billions of dollars and countless hours are spent on antiaging efforts to "stay young," in a desperate attempt to deny a natural and inevitable process.

> . . . *many older people find themselves trapped in a cruel paradox: they aspire to active aging but simultaneously dread the prospect of getting older.*

We need to embrace the term "old" and the realities of being old. But at the same time, we can be old on our own terms for as long as possible. By making choices about what it means to be old, we aren't denying time's advances, but we are taking charge of what it means to "act our age" in our own way.

The consensus among the elders we have interviewed is that young people worry too much about the pains of being old and too little about the possibilities associated with it. So, the earlier we begin to reimagine old age, the better. Geriatrician Louise Aronson, in her 2019 best seller, *Elderhood: Redefining Aging, Transforming Medicine, Reimagining Life*, writes, "We treat old age as a disease, rather than as one of three major life stages. We approach old age as a singular, unsavory entity and fail to adequately acknowledge its great pleasures or the unique attributes, contributions, physiology, and priorities of older adults. . . . As humans, we are more than the sum of our parts, but somehow as we age, we get fractionalized into being seen as a body with a disparate collection of broken parts."

A big part of the problem is that we are complicit in our own fractionalization. We pass judgment on ourselves for the signs of aging and reject ourselves accordingly. As Thomas Moore writes in *Ageless Soul: The Lifelong Journey Toward Meaning and Joy* (2017), "The first state of getting old can be unsettling. You notice stiffness in your body and wrinkles on your face. You observe that people address you differently, calling you 'ma'am' or 'sir,' or, just as typically, ignoring you altogether. You walk into a room and forget the reason you entered into it."

Small jolts like this jar us out of the illusion of youthfulness and force us to face the fact that we're getting older. These little shocks, though, are really gifts. They awaken us to the choices that aging presents; without them we'd be far less likely to step onto the path of purposeful aging.

Everyone, everywhere, is aging, whether they like it or not. With each passing moment, we're further from birth and closer to death; there's nothing we can do about that. But aging doesn't have to be passive; it can be an active process that we embrace. In other words, getting old or growing old: which will it be?

Remember when you were young and you couldn't wait to be a grown-up? You'd be able to set your own hours—no bedtimes!—and eat whatever you wanted—ice cream for breakfast!

Then you got a little older and the appeals of adulthood became more real (and expensive!): your own car and apartment, no parents telling you how to live your life, and maybe, finally, the legal right to vote or have a drink in a bar if you wanted.

What it meant to be a grown-up was pretty clear: freedom! And while some responsibility would go along with it, you'd be able to be your own person, whatever that meant to you.

No wonder you couldn't wait.

Contrast that with getting old. Chances are, it's not something you are looking forward to. In the first place, what it entails isn't nearly so clear as growing up, and in the second place, the potential promises of it aren't nearly so appealing.

So, we need to reimagine what it means to grow old, in particular by emphasizing the growing part. If the benefits of growing up include greater freedom, what do the possibilities of growing old comprise?

Traditionally, they include wisdom (debatable) and perhaps the respect of others (hard to count on) and a well-earned rest (sort of unlikely in this day and age). All of these, challenging as they may be, are fine, but in our view, the best thing about growing old is the opportunity it offers for a deeper sense of purpose in life. This results in more authentic connections with others; with oneself; and with what is sacred, or holy, or divine, however we conceive of and experience that.

This deeper sense of purpose and the connections that go along with it are fostered by a willingness to engage in honest reflection and real conversation about aging's big questions. And this requires courage.

The courageous aspect of growing old is illustrated well by the self-named Skilled Veterans Corps, a group of 200 retired engineers and other professionals over the age of 60 who volunteered to tackle the cleanup at the Fukushima nuclear plant after its meltdown following the earthquake and tsunami in Japan in 2011. It is evidenced in the spirit of the group's organizer, Yasuteru Yamada, who shared in a May 2011 interview with BBC News his belief that volunteering to take the place of younger workers at the power station was not brave but logical. He explained that at 72 years old, he figured he only had about 15 years left to live; and so, even if he were exposed to radiation, cancer, which could take 20 or 30 years to develop, was not an issue. Therefore, he reasoned, older adults like him and his fellow volunteers, with less chance of getting sick, had a greater responsibility—and ability—help out.

Although Yamada denies being brave, his willingness and ability to confront the reality of dying and do what's logical exemplifies the courage that can come to us as we grow old. It's courage squared, as it simultaneously requires the courage to look death in the face and the courage to join forces with others in service of others.

Getting Old? Or Growing Old?

As we age, we find ourselves faced with this choice: *get* old or *grow* old. Getting old is a passive, default state in which we sit back and let aging happen to us. Growing old is an active state that requires a purpose path and a practice. We say yes to the invitations and challenges of aging and no to attitudes and behaviors that no longer serve us.

> As we age, we find ourselves faced with this choice: get old or grow old.

The key to growing older is to *age from the inside out*—to reflect honestly on how aging affects the deepest parts of ourselves, who we are at our very core. It's not just about trying to be happy. As Viktor Frankl wrote in his 1946 classic, *Man's Search for Meaning*, "Happiness cannot be pursued; it must ensue. One must have a reason 'to be happy.'" He was right. We need a reason—a reason to get up in the morning, a reason to do what we do, a reason to live. We need to feel relevant, that we matter. Mattering matters. Full stop.

Chapter Two

....

If We All End Up Dying, What's the Purpose of Living?

Age can creep up on us, but then it often bursts on the scene in the form of a wake-up call, like a serious illness, the death of a loved one, the end of a long career, a decade birthday, or the kids leaving the nest. These are the moments when a sense of purpose is forged in a crucible, a severe test of who we are and who we will—as do metals in a crucible—transform into. These crucibles are the tests that launch us onto the path of purposeful aging.

Most of us will experience numerous crucibles as we age. How we make it through those crucibles and who we become as a result of them ultimately determines who we will be and the person we will grow into.

Growing old can be its own crucible, a reality captured in the popular saying "Old age ain't for sissies." It's a time of the unexpected, a new path.

Stepping onto that path begins with the recognition that at every moment in our lives, we exist somewhere between birth and death. Those are the two events we inevitably experience—although it is worth noting that the "experience" of death is not one we have in life.

Nevertheless, as we find ourselves on that timeline between our first and final breaths, we always have the potential to look back at where we've come from and forward to where we're headed. The opportunity to reflect on the past and project into the future is our choice.

Unfortunately, it's often a choice that presents itself to us as a *should*, not as something we *could* do. We lie wide awake at three o'clock in the morning, hashing over all of the mistakes and missteps we've made in our lives, flogging ourselves with the "woulda, shoulda, coulda's" from our earliest memories up to the present day. Or, we toss and turn, preparing mental lists of all the things we need to do—the changes, large and small, we have to make in our lives right now.

Or both.

It doesn't have to be this way, and for many people it isn't—at least not always. We can choose to learn from and edit our story—and in doing so, draw thoughtfully upon our memories to create a new narrative for the future.

Growing old on purpose requires being intentional about both the looking backward and the looking forward—the reflections and the projections. To do this means we grow beyond being merely a grown-up; we outgrow adulthood and grow into what we call *intentional elderhood*. But before we look forward to that, it's incumbent upon us to look backward at how we got here.

> *Growing old on purpose requires being intentional about both the looking backward and the looking forward...*

What Did I Want to Be When I Grew Up?

Think about the time some well-meaning adult asked your younger self, "What do you want to be when you grow up?"

If you were a little kid, you probably said something like "A veterinarian," "A basketball player," or "An astronaut." These generic answers are charming evidence that before we're into our teens or even early 20s, we probably have no idea about what it means to be a grown-up and have some sort of occupation. Of course, there are those rare souls who always knew what they wanted to be—artists, teachers, doctors—people born with a sense of vocation; but few of us are lucky, or driven, enough to be like that.

Your answer probably got more specific (and more realistic) by the time you entered young adulthood.

These days, most of Dave's 20-something students have a specific vocational goal in mind. They want to be software engineers or accountants, or they aspire to work at a nonprofit focused on environmental issues.

Chances are, as a young adult, like Dave's students, you were still focused on the *what* you aspired to become, the *form* rather than the *essence*. It's as if we were able to imagine the container for our lives but not really what was contained. If I'm a software engineer, you reasoned, my life will be this way; I'll *do* something and I'll *be* somebody.

When we become that *what* we aspired to, we find out that the familiar challenges remain. We may be doing the *what*, but we're still the same *who* we always were, with many of the same problems, questions, and doubts.

We may at last know *what* we are, but we still haven't addressed or discovered *who* we are. That might take some time. Usually, after having done some *what* for some time, we are able to begin discovering the *who* we were always meant (and not meant) to be.

It's typically about the third question that adults ask children when they first meet them. After "What's your name?" and "How do you like school?" comes "What do you want to be when you grow up?"

As adults, we often pose the "What do you want to be when you grow up?" question to children because it's a question that we're still asking *ourselves*.

Reflecting back on the question, therefore, can be useful in assessing how we've gotten to this place in our lives and can help us think more clearly about where we want to go from here. The reflections, in other words, are an aid to the projections.

So, ask yourself: *What did I want to be when I grew up? And how did that turn out?*

Dave reflects on the question:

"Like many of us, my first ambition was to be what my father was. When grown-ups, especially his colleagues, asked the six- or seven-year-old me what I wanted to be when I grew up, I automatically answered 'A doctor,' even though I really had no idea what that meant other than that my dad had a lab coat that he put on when I went with him to his office on weekends before we went out for Chinese food.

"By seventh grade, though, I had the whole picture sketched out in response to a 'What Do You Want to Be When You Grow Up?' assignment that my Social Studies teacher, Mrs. Ferrante, gave our class. I would go to college in New Hampshire (so I could indulge my passion for skiing as much as possible) and then become an orthopedic surgeon in Vail, Colorado (so I could make my living repairing broken bones while continuing to indulge my passion). My choice of profession had nothing to do with an interest in medicine but had everything to do with a desire to ski.

"In high school, I worked summers in the research laboratories of my dad's medical colleagues and realized that not only was I not very interested in being a physician, but I really hated spending my time in a hospital, especially with sick people!

"So, being a doctor was off the table, and what I've ended up doing—teaching philosophy and writing books—has little connection to my first ambition. The way I got here was via a pretty convoluted path, and I always have wondered if I might not have found my way more easily if I'd had a better sense, earlier on, of what my purpose was."

As we look back over our lives, when (if ever) do we begin to identify that sense of purpose Dave alludes to? Is it something we discover intentionally? Or does it emerge from any number of false starts and missteps?

The answer to those two questions is yes. Unlocking our purpose is typically an iterative process. While some people may have nailed it early on, it's much more common to determine why we're here and what we were meant to do over time. Moreover, purpose is not necessarily static. What got us up in the morning at age 20 will likely be somewhat different from what motivates us deeply when we're 60 or 70. In most cases, though, there is a connection, and looking back over our lives can help us see that.

Searching Inward for Purpose

Three simple steps can help unlock our purpose.

Step 1: Find Out How You Want to Help

When Richard launched his coaching practice, he helped anyone in any way he could. He conducted surveys, ran workshops, met in coffee shops, and spoke in church basements. This is what he knew and was good at, but parts of it didn't energize him. In fact, they were draining. As he acquired more and more clients with varying needs, he found that what he really loved to do and was good at was creating content and sharing it by writing and speaking.

So, ask yourself: *What are my gifts? What do I love to do?* To unlock our purpose, we need to figure out how we can best use the gifts we love to make a contribution to others.

Step 2: Find Out Who You Want to Help

Richard has long enjoyed the privilege of creating content and speaking to hundreds of people. He has written books that have reached more than a million readers worldwide. In doing so, he's learned that the people he's most motivated to help are those age 50 and beyond. He feels most aligned with his purpose of growing and giving when he's supporting people who want to grow old, not just get old. Most of his work now focuses on the shift from adulthood to elderhood, as in this book.

So, ask yourself: *Who do I want to help?* What pain or injustice or unhappiness have you witnessed that you just can't live with? Is there something that touches you so deeply that it keeps you up at night? There is certainly no shortage of people whom we could use our gifts to help, inspire, or support.

Step 3: Find Out What Energizes You (and What Drains You)

It's not enough to know the passion or problem you want to solve; we need to think carefully about the way that we want to solve it.

Early in Richard's career, he worked in personnel (aka human resources) at two large organizations. He was successful but restless, so he created a side hustle called Lunch Hour, Ltd.: "You buy me lunch, I coach you." He often found himself obsessing about it and creating new content for his clients. The side hustle forced him to ask himself, "What do I really want to do?" He decided that he wanted to figure out exactly why so many people died shortly after retiring. His own father was an example. So, he applied for and received a Bush Fellowship, left his job, took a second mortgage on his house, and headed to Boston, where he apprenticed on the Harvard Study of Adult Development. This experience opened his eyes to how his gifts, passions, and values fit together. He took a giant leap and opened up a coaching practice and coauthored his first book: *The Inventurers: Excursions in Life and Career Renewal.*

So, ask yourself: *What am I willing to sacrifice for?* When you discover something you're willing to sacrifice for, you know that you're onto your purpose.

Choosing to name and live our purpose is an act of courage. Ultimately, what gives our lives aliveness is living with alignment—unlocking our purpose and acting in a way that is a bold expression of who we are at our core.

Why Get Up in the Morning?

Most of us, for most of our lives, have no choice about getting up in the morning. We've got to make breakfast, hustle the kids off to school, head to work in order to make a living, keep doing what we're doing, to survive. Even on weekends, there's no time to languish in bed; chores and recreation compel us into our lives; the beat goes on and on.

Point being: we don't really have to think about our reasons for getting up in the morning; we do so because we have to, no questions asked.

This can change as we move into later life. Even if we don't retire, our daily obligations, and our appetite for meeting them, inevitably lessen. For the first time in our lives since we were little kids, we have some freedom to think about why we're getting up in the morning—or if we're going to get up at all!

What this means is that more than ever before in our lifetime, a sense of purpose becomes paramount.

Purpose is our *why*—why to get up in the morning. It's the central motivating aim that gives our life meaning. It's the answer to a question that lurks in the background of old age: "If we all end up dying, what's the purpose of living?" We need to be able to answer that question with clarity and conviction to live meaningfully in later life.

"If we all end up dying, what's the purpose of living?"

This *why* question at the core of our lives unlocks our purpose—our centering device, our compass that realigns us when we're pulled off-kilter, especially amid the dizzying changes associated with aging. Thus, the path of purposeful aging is traveled for three reasons:

First, it gives us a clear aim, an identifiable *why*—a reason to get up in the morning. In later life, we're likely to have more time to fill than we're used to; if we don't know *why* we're filling it, that time is apt to be lost. It may be filled, but we're not fulfilled.

Second, the path of purposeful aging makes us more resilient. Having a clearly identified sense of purpose helps us to reframe stressful situations so that we can deal with them more positively and bounce back more quickly.

Third, the path of purposeful aging allows us to get better as we get older. Having a sense of purpose can help us get good at growing older in these ways: real focus on real priorities, greater empathy, and heightened pattern recognition—seeing the big picture and what's important. Having a *why* fosters an optimistic outlook on life and helps keep us actively engaged in life.

Unlocking our purpose, however, is no easy, onetime task. It requires a path and a practice. Moreover, just as our bodies and minds change with age, our purpose path can (and probably will) change with age, as well. So, it's a good idea to reassess our purpose on a regular basis to ensure that we are continuing to travel our own authentic path.

And just as we are advised by our physicians and financial planners to have a regular checkup, it's advisable to do a regular purpose checkup to ensure that our answers related to purpose are still relevant. The key is practice. Any number of questions can be used, as long as we are willing to answer them honestly. Consider, as a starting point, that lurking question we posed above: "If we all end up dying, what's the purpose of living?"

Others you might explore include "What is success?" "How do you measure self-worth apart from a position and a paycheck?" "How might you give your gifts to something that is of deep interest to you and helps others?" and "If you met a younger version of yourself, what sage advice would you offer?"

The specific questions, while relevant, are not as important as our willingness to live in them over time. Just as we need to be honest with our physicians and financial planners when it comes to our regular checkups, we need to take a close look when it comes to purpose.

What Makes Me Me?

Consider the central question that has given rise to this book: "Who do I want to be when I grow old?"

It's a question we must inevitably confront in later life. If we retire, we no longer can define ourselves in terms of our work. No more are we a teacher, or businessperson, or any other specific role. With nowhere to go every morning, we may feel lost. With nothing to do, we do nothing. With no daily part to play, we lose a sense of relevance. The old adage applies: "If you are what you do, when you don't, you aren't."

As painful and disorienting as it may be, however, this situation represents an opportunity for us to choose a new reason for getting up in the morning. For many, it will be the first instance this option has ever presented itself. At last we will have the time to explore new aspects of ourselves and the world.

We spent our entire adult lives working on the *what* we wanted to be; now is the time to devote ourselves to the *who* we want to become.

> *We spent our entire adult lives working on the* what *we wanted to be; now is the time to devote ourselves to the* who *we want to become.*

In Western philosophy, there are three main solutions to the "problem of personal identity," which is a fancy name for a question that arises for all of us, especially as we age—namely, the ongoing examination of who we really are. In other words, what is our essence? What makes me "me" over time, particularly with all the changes that happen as I get older and older?

Each of the solutions has something going for it, but each falls short to some degree when confronted with the reality of what happens to us in later life.

The first solution, what philosophers typically call the "body theory," is the quite commonsensical view that our identity over time is dependent on bodily identity. It's our body that makes us who we are; as long as we have the same body, we're the same person.

But as anyone who has ever looked in a mirror after the age of 40 or so knows, this just doesn't seem right. That person staring back at me with the gray hair and wrinkles is not me; I'm really the person on the inside who looks the same as I did at 25. The face reflected toward me is an impostor, and the body that goes along with it isn't who I am at all. So, nix to the body theory.

A second solution is what is usually referred to as the "memory theory." The idea here is that what makes us who we are is a kind of psychic continuity in our mind. I'm the same person over time because I have a story—a chain of memories that leads back into my past. I can remember being 25 years old or even 15 or 10, so that's who I am, the person who has all those memories.

Again, the view stumbles when surveying the terrain in which we find ourselves as older adults, and the reason is obvious: the longer we live, the more there are events in our lives that we don't remember well. It doesn't make sense to say that just because we don't recall them, we weren't the one participating in those events. Moreover, conversely, most of us older folks remember stuff that didn't happen the way we remember it—if it happened at all—so, to the extent that our recollections of the past are, shall we say, creative, we seem not to be the person we remember ourselves to be. Thus, the memory theory doesn't carry the day.

Probably the most widely held view among the general populace is one commonly known as the "soul theory." This is the view, found in many spiritual traditions, that what makes us who we are is an immaterial soul. We are not, fundamentally, physical beings; rather, we are spiritual beings embodied in a physical form. This idea is appealing as we wonder about who we are in later life, since it means that we are not dependent on an aging body or a faulty memory. It also is comforting to many people because it holds out the promise of life after bodily death.

The main problem with the soul theory is that it's unprovable and depends on faith to accept it. We can't empirically observe our soul, and so to contend that it's my soul that makes me "me" amounts to saying, "What makes me 'me' is the thing that makes me 'me.'" True enough, but then we're still left wondering what that thing is.

All of this is to suggest that perhaps, in later life, we should take a "yes, and" perspective on the question rather than an either/or attitude. Maybe, as we think about who we are (and who we want to be) as we grow old, we can draw upon more than one way of looking at things.

With that in mind, who I am is, to some extent, my body—which helps make the case for doing my best to take care of it by exercising and eating right. But I'm also the person who remembers (and sometimes forgets or misremembers), so I should make it a point to harvest those memories, share them when appropriate, and learn from them as best I can. And finally, I'm also a soul, the details of which may be unclear but whose image reminds me that I'm more than just this physical body and the things it has done. I'm connected to something larger than myself, larger than the physical world, larger than my experience, which will continue to be after I am gone. Purpose and spirituality go hand in hand, after all.

Purposeful Aging and Spirituality

The path of purposeful aging is, ultimately, a spiritual path.

It is not, however, a path marked by self-absorbed soul-searching. On the contrary, it is a path of growing and giving. It is about recognizing and appreciating that every day we're alive is a gift. Every day we're given to live, every *today*, offers us the opportunity to choose to make a positive difference in at least one other person's life.

We may not always be able to see the effects of our actions on the lives of others, but by choosing to embrace the spirit of giving to others, we can know deep down that we are making some contribution, even a small one, to the common good. As a result, we can experience the felt sense that we make a difference, that our lives matter.

It is a natural feature of our humanity, and one that grows stronger as we age, to ponder the question, "What am I here to do?" Most spiritual traditions—Christianity, Islam, Judaism, Buddhism, Hinduism, and so on—offer a similar perspective: compassion is the soul of purpose. They teach us to love and care for our neighbors rather than focusing solely on our own needs.

The power of purpose is the power of compassion. It is the greatest of all the gifts we have to offer. Sharing this gift is the soul of spirituality.

Discovering the power of compassion in later life is another way of growing whole, not old. To grow whole is to mature spiritually.

> *The power of purpose is the power of compassion.*

Aging happens to the body; maturing spiritually happens to the soul. Aging requires nothing more than getting older; maturing spiritually requires purposeful practice.

Purpose is a verb. Aging purposefully is a spiritual practice embodied in lived day-to-day experience. If we live as a "default self"—a self hiding behind a mask of approval seeking and cultural consensus—we will always feel a sense of emptiness. We will fill our time, but it will never be fulfilling time. To age purposefully is to unmask our default self and uncover and express our true self, and that means expressing our spirituality through an expression of our purpose.

Growing whole begins with the genuine desire to connect with our true self and the greatest good within ourselves and others. As we grow whole spiritually, our lives become richer, deeper, and more compassionate.

If we live on default, without maturing spiritually, we simply get old without growing more whole. But when we live purposefully, making the conscious choice to take the path of purposeful aging, we continue to mature, grow in wisdom, and develop compassion for all living things—the essence of spirituality.

Asking ourselves, "What am I here to do today?" every day, reflecting on how to give of ourselves to others, is the embodiment of that essence and the means by which we express our spirituality in all we do, for all of our lives.

The Paradox of Aging

The connection between purpose and spirituality is well established. Now, more than ever, the role that aging plays in strengthening this bond is being researched and becoming better understood.

Mary Jo Kreitzer, PhD, RN, founder and director of the Earl E. Bakken Center for Spirituality and Healing at the University of Minnesota, is at the forefront of such research. Together with Richard, who is a senior fellow of the center, she created the Purpose Project to explore the power of purpose in integrative health and healing. She says, "At age 67, I'm glad that I don't mind getting older! With longevity comes perspective that I didn't have in my earlier years. Aging opens new insights, to reevaluate what's important."

"Aging opens new insights, to reevaluate what's important."

Her interest in purposeful aging is personal: "My mother died young, at age 62, of brain cancer. She used to say, 'I think death will be the greatest adventure.' So, I've thought about it ever since I was in my 40s. I think that death is a great teacher and, of course, the ultimate mystery. I think that I have made friends with death."

Aging can trigger a deeper existential shift. Lars Tornstam, a Norwegian sociologist, invented the term *gerotranscendence* to capture the phenomenon of how aging makes us feel less interested in material things and more interested in our inner life. Likewise, the awareness of death that comes with aging increases our focus on purpose.

Dr. Kreitzer connects aging to wholeness. "Growing whole is tapping into all aspects of life—connecting the dots. What has shifted with age is the focus of my life from achieving to mentoring and passing on wisdom. The shift to becoming an elder has required me to let go of what was and let come what is to come. And learning to live with the paradoxes of aging. My mind is vibrant and ageless, but my body has new limitations and constraints."

She accepts the challenges of aging. "One of my struggles," Dr. Kreitzer admits, "is how to answer the question, 'When are you going to retire?' I have no idea. As long as I can continue to grow and to give back, I'm going to work. I often ask myself, 'Am I missing something?' But I don't think so. Working hard has never felt easier. As director of the center, I'm an explorer creating and making natural connections. I love cultivating professional and personal relationships around the world. I guess I'm a long-life learner at heart."

It's easier to give back when we're older because we have more experiences to draw from and, perhaps, more resources to offer. But that does not account for studies showing that the choice to put purpose before personal gain in later life is just as strong regardless of income, education, or health. Dr. Kreitzer embodies this spirit as she embraces and explores new opportunities to give back as a pioneer on the frontier of the purpose movement.

Chapter Three

Aren't I Somebody?

As we age, it's not uncommon to look back on life and feel a sense of regret for things we haven't done or accomplished. Sometimes, we may even conclude that we have never really lived; we've missed out on our "real life," the life we were actually meant to live. In those pre-dawn hours, we lie in bed asking ourselves, *Is this all I'll ever be? Wasn't I meant to be somebody?*

Part of the reason for these feelings of regret is that we often set aside questions about meaning and purpose in life because we're busy living life. We go through our days by default, just doing the next thing without taking the time to wonder about why we're doing it. It's not surprising, therefore, that the questions sneak up on us and cause such consternation and worry.

Less so with Richard. He's been intrigued with the subject of purpose for as long as he can remember and has devoted his personal and professional life to exploring two key questions: "Why are we here?" and "What are we supposed to do with our time?"

"I've always wanted to know if I mattered," he says, "mattered in a way that I didn't feel like I mattered as a child. That led me to study psychology and read everything I could on the subject of purpose. And now, after decades of living, I believe I have an answer. As I've grown older (and hopefully wiser), I've come to realize that I am 'an experiment of one' penciled in for a short time, trying to make a living and make a life that matters. I've come to realize that, in fact, I am 'somebody,' not for what I've accomplished but just for who I am."

The more we're in touch with who we really are—"somebody"—the closer we come to unlocking our true purpose. When we're not trying to get somewhere or become "somebody else," it's more likely that we feel like a "real somebody."

Richard's sense of purpose inspires him to continue working full-time with no intention to retire, ever. "Still?" he says. "Sure, I'm still. I'm still writing. I'm still speaking at events around the world. I'm still doing pro bono work for projects I care about. I'm still growing and giving."

The path of purposeful aging embraces the awareness that life is constantly changing, that bad things do happen to good people, and that we have little control over many things. Learning to live with this truth, no longer trying to insist that things have to transpire in some particular way, allows us to choose to be the somebody we already are. This is not giving up but growing whole, a conscious acceptance of life as it is and in which each of us matters.

Growing whole means becoming more present. Being present feels inherently meaningful. It's meaningful because we're committed to fully experiencing our life—our "somebody-ness"—in whatever activity we're engaged in. We have the ability to choose, and that's a precious gift. Every morning is an opportunity to wake up on purpose. Every evening is an opportunity to take stock of a day well lived.

The primary reason for our existence, each and every day, is for us to grow and give. This is what we might call the "universal default purpose." This is why mattering matters.

The primary reason for our existence, each and every day, is for us to grow and give.

Into all of our lives, from time to time, come certain people whose giving helps us grow. They inspire us to expand beyond our comfort zone and become the somebody we were meant to be. Those times may be challenging, but upon reflection we realize that those were the moments in our lives when we grew more whole.

Dave cites Richard as such a person in his life. "Richard's support and mentorship has pushed me on a number of occasions over the years to step up my game as a thinker, writer, and educator—most recently as we began the writing of this book. After returning from a sabbatical in India, I hit a sort of low point where I was feeling like the best parts of my life were over, that I had peaked and accomplished all I would ever do, and that from here on out, it would pretty much be all downhill. The conversations and interactions that led to this book, however, reinvigorated me about the prospects that lie ahead. Now, I feel incredibly hopeful about what's next. Richard's gift of inspiration has made all the difference—not just for now, but for many tomorrows as well."

While the roles we play in life—parent, child, friend, author, coach, teacher, you name it—are important, they are not our life's purpose. Purpose is not a role or a goal; it is an aim and a mindset. To awaken, to grow, to continually give, and to make a difference to others—that's why we are here. It's who we bring to what we do.

> *Purpose is not a role or a goal; it is an aim and a mindset.*

Being somebody means we must remember that, in the end, we're here to grow to become the best version of ourselves. The paradox of purpose is that by being somebody (ourselves), we ultimately make the world a better place for everybody.

What else can it mean to be somebody?

Questions, Not Answers

During our adult lives, we're typically rewarded financially, emotionally, and socially for having answers. To some extent, we've grown up to be experts, or at least authorities, in our fields, and other people value us for what we know.

But the future belongs to the learners, not the knowers. So, in later life the answers become less important. The image of young people gathered around while wise elders dispense timeless wisdom is iconic but, for the most part, history. Our ability to remain relevant in the world becomes more a matter of our willingness to remain curious, to not know rather than to know, to become more than ever what Richard has modeled for many years, a true "lover of questions."

> . . . the future belongs to the learners, not the knowers.

"Always the beautiful answer who asks a more beautiful question," wrote e. e. cummings in his introduction to *New Poems* (1938). This is the spirit that has motivated Richard's work and what he considers his own small contribution to the purpose movement that he has helped pioneer.

The path of purposeful aging demands becoming a lover of questions. It means not resting easy with easy answers. Richard recalls, "I was in my late 20s when I began to wake up to my own deeper purpose questions. By societal standards, things were going well. But I was living a default life. I had found a decent way to make a decent living, but I wasn't heeding my calling. When Carl Jung pointed out that a person in his middle years without a purpose beyond himself was destined to be neurotic, he was pointing at me!"

Answers to life's questions are critical, but those answers must continually lead to more questions. When we stop questioning, we stop growing. We begin living by default, which leads to what we call "inner kill," the act of dying from the inside out.

Heeding our calling—which becomes a more important choice as we age—requires that we ask ourselves why we're doing what we're doing, that we explore ourselves more deeply than ever. The later years of our lives present us with a unique opportunity for such exploration. And the key to such exploration remains, until our last breath, more questions.

Close Encounters of the Old Kind

The title of Steven Spielberg's classic science fiction film from 1977, *Close Encounters of the Third Kind,* refers to the US Air Force's *Project Blue Book* alien-encounter classification system. A close encounter of the first kind is sighting of a UFO, the second kind is physical evidence to prove the existence of an alien, and the third kind is actual contact with alien life forms.

We might see our own encounters with aging as falling into a similar taxonomy: a close encounter of the first kind would be seeing the signs of aging; of the second kind, feeling them; and of the third kind, coming to grips with the "alien" life form we have become as an old person. But, as in the film, this third kind of encounter is where transformation takes place. It's where we learn the most—if not, as in the film, the ultimate secrets of the universe, at least the ultimate truths about ourselves.

In preparing for this book, we've investigated encounters of that third kind through interviews and conversations with people whom we and others have identified as being on the path of purposeful aging. We've structured those conversations around a key inquiry: "Who do you want to be as you grow old? What does the good life mean to you as you grow into elderhood? And how are you living that life?"

The answers we've received to that inquiry have informed our writing, as have less formal encounters of the old kind, like the one Richard recounts here:

"Recently, I had a 55-year-reunion lunch with my former high school tennis partner, Bob Weinstine, and it gave rise to a kaleidoscope of emotions and remembrances. Bobby, who grew up to be a founding partner of one of the Midwest's most prestigious law firms, and I shared our stories of careers, divorce, remarriage, children, and grandchildren. We identified the crucible events that had forged our personalities and attitudes about the world. I learned of the grief that Bob was carrying over the loss of his son—a hole in his heart never to heal.

"He shared with me his reminiscences of the 50th high school reunion. He recalled the endless 'organ recitals' as old acquaintances bemoaned the state of their hearts, or lungs, or kidneys, or livers, or prostates. Information on how to find a good hearing aid or a reliable assisted living space was exchanged. Unexpected destinies were recounted: one former star athlete became a well-known federal judge; another great athlete committed suicide. All this was well and good, but it wasn't until the conversation turned to death and dying that things really got interesting.

"Bob pulled out the 'memorial list,' and it brought gasps and tears to both of us, not only for the friends we had lost, but for those we now would never have the chance to know.

"It made me reflect on my experience of giving the eulogy some years ago for our classmate, my best friend growing up. We stayed close from kindergarten until his final breath. The words I spoke at his memorial service, the tears I shed over his loss, remain with me to this day. Strange how death quickly brings to life feelings buried alive.

"Perhaps the theme of any 50th high school reunion should be the many paths of purposeful and purposeless aging—the paths we all took from the 25th reunion, when we were still 'masters of the universe,' to the 50th, when we were more transparent, vulnerable, and aging with or without purpose.

"I left the lunch with Bob pleased that I've spent most of my professional life studying for the age we've become. Yet, even so, I find the condition deeply paradoxical, filled as it is with both distress and discovery.

"I recall the last lines of Carl Jung's autobiography, *Memories, Dreams, Reflections* (1963), 'I'm astonished, disappointed, pleased with myself. I'm distressed, depressed, rapturous. I'm all these at once, and cannot add up the sum.'

"The same goes for me. I'm happy just to be alive. At the same time, I embrace the cosmic joke that the best teacher about life turns out to be death. At any moment, we might breathe out our last breath; it can come at any time. That closeness to death makes life all the much sweeter."

The reunion lunch reminded Richard that on the way to his original career aspiration of becoming a wilderness camp director, he ended up here, as an author, keynote speaker, life coach, and tireless questioner into matters of meaning and purpose. His journey to this point was shaped by the questions he asked (and was asked) along the way.

The Stories of Our Lives

Looking back on our lives, as Richard's 50th-reunion story illustrates, helps us to glean lessons for the path of purposeful aging. So, it's useful to keep in mind that famous quote, usually attributed to Mark Twain, that Dave's mom, Ruth Shapiro, adopted as her own: "Never

let the facts get in the way of a good story." Ruth's stories were like those movies "based on actual events,"
with the emphasis on "based on." It used to sometimes
drive his father, a scientist for whom facts and data were
paramount, absolutely nuts. For Dave's dad, details mattered. The day of the week, the city in which it occurred,
the actual words that people said, were important. For
his mom, though, it was the essence of the thing—the
message or moral that the story communicated, what it
revealed about the people involved—that was key.

As we age, and the details of our former lives tend to
get somewhat murkier, we might move in the direction
of the Ruth Shapiro approach to storytelling. The specif-
ics of what happened can recede into the background a
bit; we can tell the story of our life to others (and ourselves) with greater emphasis on what we learned from
an event and what it tells us about who we are and the
people with whom we are connected. Less important is
whether it happened on a Tuesday or a Wednesday, or in
New York or Chicago, or even who said what, than why it
happened and what we learned from it.

The world turns on stories. Sharing our stories is
among the most important ways
we connect with others in the later
years of our lives. But, of course,
there's a continuum, with one end
being "that boring old person who
tells the same stories over and over

> *Sharing our stories is among the most import-ant ways we connect with others in the later years of our lives.*

again" and the other being "that fascinating elder who shares their unique wisdom with every tale they tell." We will all fall along that continuum somewhere at some points; the goal is to skew toward the latter whenever possible. One key to that is keeping in mind the reason we're storytelling. If it's to authentically connect with our audience, then we're probably on the right track; if it's all about just reliving the past, maybe not so much.

Ruth Shapiro's best stories—and she had many—were ones that revealed her own character in all its odd glory and illustrated her skewed outlook on the strangeness of the world we inhabit. Even when she was talking about her favorite subject—herself—she always managed to make it relevant for her listeners, much to their delight and (often) consternation.

So, as we think about looking back on our lives and telling ourselves and others the stories that enable us to make sense of who we've become, it behooves us to keep in mind who the stories are for. Even stories about us are not entirely about us. In telling them, we connect with others, and in doing so, we connect with ourselves.

An Inspired Life

When Tom Schreier graduated from Notre Dame more than three decades ago, he never dreamed that in his late 50s he'd be back at his alma mater, as founder and director of the university's Inspired Leadership Initiative. But, captivated at midlife by the challenge of helping others to make the retirement transition that he himself was making, Tom returned; and now, in addition to directing the Initiative, he teaches a class called Designing an Inspired Life.

He reflects on how this transpired: "When I was done with my career, I wasn't done. But what could I do? I was only 55 years old and I was hungry for a fresh calling. I yearned for a compass that would guide me to the next phase of my life."

Purpose provided that compass. It pointed Tom in the direction he sought as he graduated from adulthood to elderhood, much as it had when he graduated from college. "At Notre Dame," he says, "we were encouraged to explore what matters most to us, to discern our calling, and by later life, we'd have it all sorted out. Not true, however. For me, I retired at age 55 and was adrift. Suddenly, I woke up in the morning without a compass to guide my next phase of life. Purpose became more urgent for me when I faced retirement. I had to slow down, reflect, and reimagine my life. I had to let go of my prior identity to be in a state of constant transformation. I needed to figure out my limitations and revise my expectations and, thus, my measure of success and failure, accordingly. I call this my 'purpose compass.'"

His purpose compass led him straight toward service to others. "What intrigues me is to have a meaningful impact on the people who then have a meaningful impact on others. My purpose now is to help people find their moral compass—their purpose—by providing the best tools and mentors to help them live their best possible life. I'm inspired to help people go through the discover and discernment process to uncover who they are really meant to become next. There's a lot of potential freedom in 'becoming'—intellectual, emotional, and time freedom." But, as Tom has seen, this freedom, especially later in life, can be frightening, particularly when people are unsure of how to exercise it.

Having good role models is an important way to discern next steps, Tom observes. "One of my mentors was a colleague with a clear moral compass—Paul Karos. Paul brought purpose to Wall Street and beyond. He helped me understand that even on Wall Street, there is a deeper bottom line beyond the obvious bottom line. In spite of having lost his eyesight and becoming legally blind, Paul has recast his own aging from decline to discernment, from self to service."

Through his efforts with the Inspired Leadership Initiative , Tom has found fulfillment as a result of his own growing and giving. His inspired life is an ongoing inspiration to others.

Chapter Four

Am I Living the Good Life My Whole Life?

A fundamental question on the path of purposeful aging is, "What is the good life?"

With that question and related inquiries into whether we are living our conception of it, we continue the real conversation with ourselves and loved ones that enables us to age purposefully. This conversation is informed deeply by our cultural experience—by the way we grew up and the models of aging that were presented to us. At the same time, there is a universality to the patterns and practices of youth and later life, as we can see by observing traditions other than those we were raised in.

For example, in the traditional Hindu conception of life, people move through four age-based stages known as *ashramas*. (To be historically accurate, this model pertains only to men and mainly to the Brahmin or priestly caste, but for our purposes we can usefully apply it to everyone.)

First, there is the student (*brahmacharya*) stage, in which one devotes their life to study with a guru. Next comes the householder (*grihastha*) stage, in which one works and raises a family. Subsequently, after one's children are grown up and have families of their own, a person moves into the "retiring to the forest" (*vanaprastha*) stage, in which worldly concerns about making money and pursuing pleasure become secondary to seeking spiritual liberation. Finally, near the end of one's life, a person enters into the "renunciate" (*sannyasa*) stage, where traditionally one gives up all their possessions and dedicates their life entirely to spiritual pursuits.

The first two stages correspond pretty closely to how most of us in the contemporary world conceive of our lives. We first go to school and then get a job. If we're lucky, we work in a field we've studied for, and if all goes according to plan, this includes a satisfying home life.

But things diverge a bit when it comes to life after a career—what is commonly called "retirement." The contemporary conception of later life is not really a period of spiritual engagement. The more common cultural notion is that it's a time for savoring life, a time that marks the passage from a life of work to a life of liberation, leisure, and sleeping late. Sure, there are "active agers" who take art or dance classes or volunteer, but still the focus is outward, with an emphasis on doing things and staying busy—a far cry from the idea that later life is when we ought to focus on becoming enlightened.

We might ask ourselves, though, given the less-than-ideal experience of many people in their later years, whether we might learn something from the traditional Hindu model. In particular, does it make sense to conceive of one's late life as less of a reward for having engaged in paid work for so many years and more of an opportunity to engage in the personal work of spiritual growth? And if so, how can this exploration of our spiritual self enable us to more successfully live the good life for our whole life?

In *Repacking Your Bags*, we defined the good life as "living in the place you belong, with people you love, doing the right work, on purpose." We have slightly modified that definition for later life to be "living in the place you belong, with people you love, doing spiritual work, on purpose." How, then, are we to define "spiritual work"?

> . . . "living in the place you belong, with people you love, doing spiritual work, on purpose."

Our definition of spiritual work, as discussed earlier, is quite inclusive. It includes traditional practices like prayer, meditation, contemplation of relevant scriptures, and communing with nature, but it also comprises purposeful activities like helping others and working on behalf of a better world. The key is that it connects us to something that is larger than and beyond ourselves and is consistent with an understanding of what's sacred. "God is one; his names and forms are many" is how the Vedantic monk and scholar Swami Vivekananda put it. We can find our way to the divine via any number of paths. It does require work—work we're likely to have more time for in later life—but the specific details of that work are up to each of us.

The only litmus test is to ask ourselves whether the practice, whatever form it takes, is moving us toward a closer connection to what we take to be sacred. This doesn't, by the way, commit us to believing in God; it simply is based on a more universal recognition that life is a sacred mystery and that the embrace of this mystery is an undeniable component of what it truly means to be human.

Unpacking the Good Life

One of the most enduring questions in the history of philosophy is "What is the good life?" The best-known ancient Greek philosophers—Socrates, Plato, and Aristotle—all took it on, as did Stoics like Marcus Aurelius and Epictetus; and the question dominates other philosophical traditions, such as those of India and China, as well. We even weighed in with our own thoughts on the matter in our first book, *Repacking Your Bags*. It's a question that's endlessly intriguing across time and place; and with more than 7 billion people on the planet, there are probably 6.999 billion different answers to it.

Part of this diversity of views is due to the difficulty of getting agreement on what a good life is. For some, it's pleasure. For others, wealth. Still others reckon the good life in terms of power or popularity. Aristotle rejected all three of these common conceptions in favor of a view that essentially held the good life to be the most virtuous life. Plato argued, more or less, that the life of philosophical contemplation was best. In Vedic and Buddhist traditions, the good life is one that results in spiritual liberation.

Whatever the definition, one thing most everyone agrees on is that a good life is desirable. No one, except perhaps masochists, wants to live a bad life (and for masochists, a bad life would be a good life, so perhaps there are no exceptions).

As we unpack the good life, particularly in later years, in order to live the good life for our whole life, some common themes emerge. Paramount among these is living a life that sets us free—however we conceive of freedom. This results in a life that brings self and service to life. Crucial to this is a felt sense of compassion, of wanting to make a contribution to something larger than oneself, rather than feeling that it's something one ought to do. *Purpose* is a verb; it is a path and a practice.

A good life in later life is one whose waning moments are not wasted on mundanities. Instead, it focuses more on what really matters and at the same time contributes to our own growth and fulfillment. Such a life requires self-awareness. Living a good life in later life is an inner journey, a path that leads to finding our highest self in the act of serving others.

How to Worry Well

When Richard speaks from the podium, he often makes the point that "three Ms"—money, medicine (health), and meaning (purpose)—are equally important to living a good life in later life. Most of his audience—and society in general—tends to fixate on the first "M," however.

Richard has observed time and again that the number one question occupying people's minds about aging is, "Will I have enough money to live the 'good life' you speak of?" Moreover, he's also seen, just as often, that the number one reason people give for not living the good life late in life is that they don't have enough money to do so.

This is real. But it's wrong.

Money is essential, of course. And not having enough to pay one's bills—especially, for older folks, medical bills—is a serious problem for far too many. But for the majority of us, it's the perception of "enough" that plays a bigger role in the degree to which we experience the good life in later life. It's not how much we have, really; it's how we feel about how much we have and how that affects the choices we make.

We've all known people who have money but are unhappy; and more to the point, we've all known people who don't have money but are happy.

So, what's the point? Worry about money is part of living a longer life. Living on a fixed income might make us feel anxious. Seeing the mountain (relatively speaking) of one's finances steadily decrease each month toward a molehill can be a source of understandable concern. Five minutes into any conversation about money with men and women over 60, and almost inevitably fears of homelessness and abandonment emerge.

The path of purposeful aging is not to deny these concerns; it's not about "Don't worry, be happy." It's about how to "worry well." To worry well means, first, to be clear about our vision of the good life, and second, to be clear about how much is enough to live that vision.

> To worry well means, first, to be clear about our vision of the good life, and second, to be clear about how much is enough to live that vision.

And yet, it's commonplace for people to believe they need more in order to be happy. Because money is so emotionally charged, lack of money is often the first line of defense to explain why we can't make changes to our lives or why we're not living what we believe to be the good life. It can be a convenient avoidance mechanism, a way to make excuses to ourselves for not being satisfied with the life that we're living.

As we've mentioned earlier, the *vanaprastha* stage of life, those years of deeper spiritual inquiry that follow our lives as working people, is one in which acquisition of things becomes less important than acquiring a deeper understanding of connection to the sacred and the divine. While contemporary life doesn't typically afford us the ability to retire to the forest for spiritual study with the sages, it can be useful to keep this model in mind in later life. We may do well to reel in our desires for more stuff and instead adopt an attitude of finding satisfaction from within.

True wealth, as the old adage goes, is not about having what we want; it's about wanting what we have.

Most of us, for most of our lives, have accepted the principle "Time is money." Thus, we seek efficiency, productivity, and action as means to greater riches. But in later life, the equation changes to "Money is time." Our most valuable currency is the time we have left to spend. The simple fact that people will spend fortunes to extend their lives even briefly is proof of time's value.

Spending our precious currency—time—in ways that are meaningful and fulfilling is what makes us feel wealthy. Being able to give of ourselves to others—family, friends, strangers in need—is what makes that time meaningful. The more of ourselves that we give away—the more generous our actions—the richer we become.

The Native American peoples of the Pacific Northwest had a tradition known as the potlatch, which was a ceremonial distribution of property and gifts to affirm or reaffirm social status. A tribal leader's wealth was reckoned in terms of how much they were willing and able to give away. In later life, we may do well to adopt and adapt this tradition as our own. Instead of material wealth, the gifts of ourselves that we bestow upon others—our lessons learned, our kindness, and our gratitude, for example—are the true markers of our prosperity.

There are any number of ways to communicate values and life lessons from one generation to the next, apart from the simple practice of sharing them in person. Many people have used ethical wills, legacy letters, or living legacy videos as a means to share their messages.

Thus, the question "How much is enough?" is more easily answered: as much of ourselves as we are able and willing to give.

Purpose and a Paycheck

The story is commonplace: a life of energy and engagement in the first half, followed by decline and disengagement in the second half. You know them: older, feeling invisible and irrelevant. As Chris Farrell, author and nationally syndicated economics contributor, says, "They landed in limbo after a lifetime of achievement. Millions of older adults are living in financial limbo. Financial anxiety is not just a boomer phenomenon. Gen Xers and millennials are not going to have pensions either. And they're going to have to work for 60 or 70 years!"

Yet, according to Farrell, the core of personal finance is not money. The foundation of prosperity in later life is exploring our values and learning how we want to live our life. And the word that best captures that exploration of values is *purpose*.

In his 2019 book *Purpose and a Paycheck: Finding Meaning, Money, and Happiness in the Second Half of Life*, Farrell recalls the wisdom of the legendary writer and broadcaster Studs Turkel on how important a sense of purpose is to people in all walks of life. In his 1974 best seller *Working: People Talk about What They Do All Day and How They Feel about What They Do*, Turkel interviewed people who recounted the hardships, disappointments, joys, and satisfactions they experienced in their daily labors. He chronicled the connection that arises from work—the dignity in a job well done and the sense of community that comes from working together with others.

Turkel summarized what he learned: "It is about search, too, for daily meaning as well as daily bread, for recognition as well as cash, for astonishment rather than torpor."

Chris Farrell similarly summarizes what he has learned as a journalist interviewing countless people over decades of work: "The search for purpose and a paycheck is widely shared. We have different goals, values, and talents, but we share the desire to know that what we are doing matters." He advises that "wise financial planning is grounded in finding a purpose. Financial planning is best thought of as money-management to support the purpose journey. A financial plan is a road map to help you achieve your goals." Primary among those goals for everyone is connection with others.

He goes on to clarify: "We put enormous value on things, when what we truly value are experiences. 'What is my "number" to retire on?' is the wrong way think about it. First, ask 'What is it I really want to do?' then figure out the money component. If you're going from money to what you want to do, you'll never get there. Start with what you truly value. Also, know what you don't want to do. With aging comes the experience of being able to clearly say 'no.'" "No," it turns out, is a complete sentence.

Farrell advises that a critical ingredient to add to the personal finance mix is real conversation. You need to talk about money and purpose with closest friends and committed listeners. He also advocates for the "unexpected meeting" that can shift one's mindset about new possibilities from doom and gloom to "I could do that!"

Opening ourselves up to meeting new people can come from volunteering, from joining a book club or study group, or from leisure activities that bring us into real conversation with others. "The combination of giving and conversation allows for the kind of intentional lifestyle experimentation and thoughtful work transitions that turn purpose into reality," Farrell says.

And as Farrell's work reminds us, it's never too late to do so; in fact, there's no better time than the second half of life.

Chapter Five

....

How Do I Stop Living
a Default Life?

The choice that's the absence of a choice is the *default choice*—as in online shopping where the default choice is having your billing address and your shipping address be the same. Default choices are useful because they promote efficiency. No need to make a decision when we don't really have to; just proceed by default and get on with things.

But while the default choice may be the way to go for simple things in life like online shopping, it's less than ideal as an overall approach to life itself. Just floating along from one year to the next, accepting things as they present themselves without question or intention, is a surefire recipe for dissatisfaction and despair in later life.

Living the default life is living a life that's ultimately inauthentic and impersonal; it's living a life that isn't really of our own choosing. It's living a life that inevitably gives rise to questions like "Where did all the time go?" "How did my life pass so quickly?" and "Why did I squander my one precious opportunity for living?"

Living the default life is living a life that's ultimately inauthentic and impersonal; it's living a life that isn't really of our own choosing.

We often unconsciously live our lives by default; in fact, that's a big part of what it means to do so. When Richard was growing up in the late 1950s and early 1960s, the default version of adulthood was unquestioned: you were done with your education and settled into a job or career that paid the bills. You found a mate, got married, and bought a small starter home; you were on your own at last! Oh, and all this before you turned 25. The default path to becoming a grown-up was short and direct—and usually for life.

Many people didn't take this short and direct path, but it was overwhelmingly the norm. You checked the default boxes: education or training, a steady job, marriage, kids, a second car, etc.; being a grown-up was a matter of accomplishing a set of predetermined milestones. There were exceptions, of course, but they were exceptions that, by and large, proved the rule.

Today, there are many more exceptions to becoming a grown-up. These days, adulthood is more of a choice than a set path with specific milestones. Outward markers have lost the power to entirely define our options.

Along with this is, not surprisingly, a similar shift in what it means to be old. The traditional milestones of old age—retirement, the death of one's parents, grandchildren, etc.—are no longer definitive of what it means to be old. Now, it's more about choices; we're freer now to decide for ourselves what being old means and how we intend to live our later years. But that requires us to confront default choices and reject easy answers. It means honestly exploring tough questions like "Am I really living my life or someone else's version of it?" and "What's missing in my life?"

Richard routinely asks workshop participants to share their biggest challenge in the second half of life. This finding emerges: Nearly everyone has considerable issues—not just the usual health and financial challenges of aging, but the types that have persisted for years, that have become themes in people's lives, issues like "making the best of it," feeling "invisible," the sense of being an "impostor," or the fear of having missed out on life's opportunities with no time left to catch up.

It's pretty typical for participants to feel that something big is missing. To the extent that this is a result of having lived a default life is up for review, but there's no doubt that many of us find ourselves at a point where what's missing can no longer be overlooked. We're wondering how to fill that hole in our heart before our most precious currency—time—is completely spent.

Upon further reflection, workshop participants typically agree that the missing component is not a function of having avoided pain; death and suffering are facts of life. Rather, what seems to be lacking can be narrowed down to an unexamined aspect of one or more factors that contribute to people's experience of the good life: These are *place* (where they live), *people* (who they spend their time with), *life work* (what they do all day, every day), and *purpose* (why they do what they do).

This sense of something missing, which people of any age may feel, can usually be traced to one of these four areas. And the reason for that emptiness, more often than not, is that people have opted to live a default life. Moving from the default life to the good life, therefore, is a matter of becoming intentional about place, people, life work, and/or purpose.

From a Default Life to a Good Life

As Richard's workshop participants illustrate, it's common, especially in the second half of life, to feel that something is missing or unsettled. That feeling is often due to a mismatch between a default life and a good life as an individual conceives it. And it's exacerbated by feelings of fear or inadequacy to address that mismatch.

Do I settle? Or do I make a move to change? Choosing to change just one of the four areas is likely to result in a significant shift in attitude. Things might get better or they might get worse, at least initially; we can never know until the change is made. This uncertainty is enough to keep people stuck in default living—especially in later life, when those default choices are so ingrained.

Moreover, for many people, the very idea of making conscious choices about these major life structures is pretty foreign; typically, we didn't initially choose our place, our people, our life work, and our purpose; they chose us!

Where is my true place?

Our place, where we live, is typically the most common default choice, and yet it may have the biggest effect of all, since in many ways it determines all the rest. We're born somewhere we didn't choose; we grow up there, and we stay. If we move, it's often not really a "choice"; it's for a job, or a relationship, or to go to school. Of course, some people do set off somewhere new in hopes of finding happiness or adventure, but they're in the minority— and recent statistics show that minority is shrinking. So, most of us settle into place by default and become too settled to seriously consider moving.

Who are my real people?

People—our family, for sure, but also friends and acquaintances—are often in our lives as defaults. The people in our lives are usually the people who have happened to become the people in our lives. They were the people around us as we grew up, got jobs, moved into neighborhoods, and started families. How many of us make great new friends later in life? It's possible but unusual. Our scope of relationships, in fact, often narrows. Once we're settled in our relationships, we become complacent and stop actively looking for friends who strongly resonate with our values and interests—if we ever did so at all. We withdraw once again and settle.

What is my life work?

Our work, what we end up spending the majority of our lifetime doing, often depended on what we saw as our options when we were starting to enter the working world. We went with what our parents or teachers recommended or whatever seemed to make sense at the time or simply what paid the bills. The result—decades spent making a living in some way—is more or less happenstance by default. We didn't choose our work; it chose us. In later life, it's often the same story. Our later-life work might be volunteer, paid, unpaid, creative hobbies, or entrepreneurship; the majority of people don't or can't retire. But to the extent that those options have chosen us, we're working by default.

What is my "why"—my purpose?

Our purpose, our vital sense of why we're doing all this, anyway, is often the least-examined aspect of our lives. Very few of us consciously choose our purpose until faced with a crisis, which is why so many people, especially in later life, find themselves, like the participants in Richard's workshops, feeling that sense of missing something big.

If we accept the premise that living a purposeful life is preferable to living a default life, why is it that so many people grow up without intentionally choosing the life they want? Fear is the major deterrent: fear of contradicting the default expectations of others, fear of being broke, fear of taking a stand as an individual, and perhaps most of all, fear of confronting feelings of isolation.

We've all seen the Hallmark card/bumper-sticker slogan, "Today is the first day of the rest of your life." Perhaps a more relevant way of putting it would be "Today is the last day of my life, and I'm going to live it as if I don't have any more."

> "Today is the last day of my life, and I'm going to live it as if I don't have any more."

Overcoming our fears and choosing not to settle is a great challenge of later life. So much of our earlier life consists of conditions we've fallen into and made the best of. We gravitate unconsciously toward what's comfortable. When we choose to grow old, though (rather than merely get old), is when we can step back and see where we've come from, to finally live our own version of a good life.

Richard has interviewed hundreds of people over the age of 65 and asked them, "If you could live your life over again, would you change anything?" Often the answer is no, because not all the choices they've made by default are bad choices; many, if not most, are consistent with their values. But what are the odds that all the defaults delivered to us by happenstance are completely consistent with what's optimal for our whole life?

The something big that's missing, described by both Richard's interviewees and his workshop participants, is a result of their having gone with the default life for much too long. Listen, as Richard does, to those who do make those changes, though, and you'll hear them say afterward, "I'm now in a much better place in my life; I don't know how I lived that old way for so long."

The secret to ending default living is really no secret at all: Be yourself—full stop. That means not being dependent on the approval of others but, rather, consciously choosing to be your own person, on purpose, not by default.

> *The secret to ending default living is really no secret at all: Be yourself—full stop.*

A "Sparked Life"

In his 1998 book *A Year to Live: How to Live This Year as If It Were Your Last*, Stephen Levine observes that, against all odds, "when people know they are going to die, that last year is often the most loving, most conscious, and most caring."

Joel Theisen, age 52 and a nurse by training and background, agrees. "I've lived through that year with so many people. As a nurse, it often felt like I wasn't able to provide the value that I wanted to bring to people.

I wanted to bring smiles back to their faces, to bring a spark back to their eyes."

So, Theisen created Lifespark (originally Lifesprk), a whole-person senior services provider working to change people's experience of their final years. He says, "Our purpose is to create a meaningful experience that allows older adults to maintain their purpose, passions, and social well-being as they age—to live what I call a 'sparked life.'"

Theisen subscribes to the common wisdom that life is what you make of it. "I created Lifespark to help seniors make the most of their lives." With decades of home care experience, he realized that the missing piece in a sparked life was purpose; his patients yearned not just to live, but to live with passion and meaning. "To live a sparked life, we need a reason to get up every day," he explains. "I want to be a teacher to free up the human spirit. That's my purpose, my reason to get up in the morning. I want to get a passing grade for freeing up the human spirit of as many people as I can touch. In fact, I want to move our whole-person approach to transform the health care industry."

Theisen has created the Lifespark Experience—a whole-person approach centered on a customized Life Plan. This sparks elders by inspiring them to be fearless in their pursuit of their passions and purpose. And in fact, this approach is waking up the industry, by reducing emergency room visits by 52 percent and hospitalizations by 73 percent, and even lowering long-term health care costs. That alone gives Theisen far more than a passing grade, but more important, as he says, "it's helping seniors to live longer, healthier, happier, more independent lives."

Does greater longevity really matter? "Yes," according to Theisen, "but it only matters if we make it purposeful, if our spirits are alive and contributing to life. I try to surround myself with those who I feel are aging well. And I do two things to age well myself. First, I slow down and put myself in places that demand quiet and that breathe into me a sense of wholeness. And second, I love to spend time listening to the stories of our elder clients, to learn how they have earned a passing grade. It helps me to grow more whole—to be a kinder soul—to learn to be a better teacher on purpose."

Chapter Six

Am I Having a Late-Life Crisis?

We've all heard the inspirational quote, "There's a reason your windshield is bigger than your rearview mirror; where you're headed is more important than what you've left behind." But for many people in later life, it's all about that mirror.

Countless numbers of elders—and probably most of us at some time during later life—are way more focused on what's in the rear view than on what's ahead. This is not necessarily a problem, but if it prevents us from dealing with—or even really seeing—what's on the horizon, it can be a sign of what has come to be known as the *late-life crisis*.

The late-life crisis, like its more famous younger sibling, the midlife crisis, really is a thing. Recent research has found that as many as one in three people over the age of 60 will experience it in some form.

The late-life crisis is characterized by dissatisfaction; a loss of identity; an expectations gap; and the feeling that life has peaked, so it's all downhill from here.

Whereas the midlife crisis is typically about the loss of opportunities, the late-life crisis is more about the loss of relevance. Stereotypically, during the midlife crisis, you dye your hair and buy a sports car; during the late-life crisis, it feels pointless to even get out of your bathrobe.

> *Whereas the midlife crisis is typically about the loss of opportunities, the late-life crisis is more about the loss of relevance.*

Also, unlike the midlife crisis, which popular culture and the punchlines of late-night comedians tell us is mostly a guy thing, the late-life crisis is not gender-specific. Women and men seem equally likely to experience it.

The particulars of the crisis can be hard to pin down. Is it a time of massive change and reprioritization? A mysterious chasm between the past and the future? Or just a normal sad and panicky feeling of anxiety in response to the challenges of aging? In a word, yes to all of those.

The late-life crisis can be triggered by a crucible event. The death of a loved one, an illness, money problems, or even something as simple as no longer being able to complete that favorite hike or bend into that particular yoga pose can set it off. Or, it can simply be the mind-draining drudgery of more of the same. One day we're an "active ager" embracing the experience of later life; the next we're decrepit, feeling invisible and irrelevant.

Of course, outward changes acknowledged, the real crisis is taking place on the inside. Our response to the inevitable changes brought on by age is what determines whether we'll experience crisis or have the mindset to reimagine our future. Will we get stuck in the past and overwhelmed by morbid thoughts about the end of life? Or will we draw upon past lessons and learning and focus instead on how to make the most of the rest of our life?

Part of the answer has to do with how we've lived up until the crisis point. If we generally feel fulfilled by a life well spent, we're apt to have the mindset to glance back in the rearview mirror with satisfaction and to look forward through the windshield with hope. But if we're in the midst of a long arc of dissatisfaction that has been simmering for some time, we're more apt to feel despair when faced with limited years and what we take to be limited possibilities ahead.

Naturally, we all have days when we look in the mirror (figuratively as well as literally) and don't particularly like what we see. "Who have I become?" we ask. "Who is this person in the mirror? And what are my real possibilities?" Such feelings are not necessarily a sign of the late-life crisis, but if they linger and really get in the way of our experience of living, they might be.

Most of us go through periods in our lives when we feel like something's missing, when it seems like we're off course or lack direction. But the late-life crisis is different. In the late-life crisis, we feel the clock ticking.

One thing is certain, however: the degree to which we are able to admit being in the late-life crisis determines the degree to which we'll be able to move through it. Asking ourselves a series of questions, like those that follow, can help us to see whether we're experiencing a crisis.

1. Do you often find yourself looking in the mirror and thinking, "Who is this person?"

2. Do you feel reluctant to tell people your age?

3. Do you obsess about your appearance, trying to "antiage," to look younger?

4. Do you often compare yourself with others your age (and worry that you're not measuring up)?

5. Do you often find yourself thinking about your mortality?

6. Do you avoid discussing with your loved ones what you would like for them after you're gone?

7. Do you often question the value of your religious or spiritual beliefs?

8. Do you often feel down or empty for long periods of time?

9. Do you often feel detached from activities that once gave you pleasure?

10. Do you feel bored or stuck in your personal relationships?

You might relate to a few of these behaviors, thoughts, and feelings. But if you answered a definite "yes" to more of the questions than you answered "no" to, it's possible that you are in (or entering into) a late-life crisis.

So, what can you do if you know that you're in (or on the cusp of) a late-life crisis? How can you successfully move forward?

It is useful to frame the crisis in a new way. We've all heard that apparently apocryphal claim that the Chinese term for *crisis* is roughly translated as "danger plus opportunity." While that may be linguistically in error, the message is absolutely on point.

The late-life crisis is an opportunity for us to reframe what it means to get old—to change our mindset from danger to opportunity, from living a default life to living a good life. This means choosing how to see a new image in the mirror.

Instead of looking back and lamenting our losses and what we never did, we can gaze in the rearview mirror and see the lessons we can learn from it. Reflection on the past can be an opportunity for growth—a chance to draw upon our past experiences in order to apply that insight to the future. Instead of living life in the rear-view mirror, focused on "shoulds" (I should have worked harder, loved better, learned more, earned more), we can live for the windshield and practice more of the "coulds" (I could work harder, love better, learn more, and so on) from here on out.

The late-life crisis is an opportunity for us to acknowledge that we're challenged with naturally arising emotions and complex choices that are common to aging, and that we need to have real conversation with family, friends, and others to meet those challenges. We need to be able to be honest with others about what we're feeling.

Key to avoiding or managing a late-life crisis is to not go it alone; isolation is fatal.

Key to avoiding or managing a late-life crisis is to not go it alone; isolation is fatal.

Renewing Hope through Crisis

Nothing forces us to face what must be changed like crisis.

The COVID-19 pandemic, the senseless murder of George Floyd—these crises might leave us feeling hopeless, but by facing that hopelessness, we may find a renewed sense of purpose and greater hope within.

Tracy Hudson, an artist based in Minnesota's Twin Cities, is a case in point. She wrote to Richard, "Before the pandemic began, I had recently rented an art studio to do my painting and to offer classes. Well, plans change. COVID-19, I break my foot while gardening, and George Floyd's precious life was lost. So, while there would be no marching for me, my daughter and I started painting banners in support of Black Lives Matter with large portraits of George Floyd on them. I did what you encourage; I leaned into my gifts and passions to see what I had to offer. . . . We feel helpless when we sit and do nothing, but the only person making us sit and do nothing is ourselves."

With nowhere to go and her classes canceled, Hudson found the time to do things she had often been too busy to do: Read. Have real conversations. Rethink life. Paint on purpose.

The racial justice crisis galvanized her sense of purpose: "To not be afraid to see, to feel, and to express energy." And it has enabled her to focus her energy in ways that serve herself and others.

Purpose does that. As Hudson says, "Painting is my Zen where I lose all track of time. No matter what circumstances I face, I have to have faith that I'll have a 'why' to get up for."

Purpose gives us a compelling *why*. It helps us tap into our reserves—our gifts and passions—that might be dormant.

A forced pause like the one that Hudson faced has forced many of us to take a deeper look at how we're "doing life." Her art reflects the effort to live purposefully.

This is the path of choosing to align the deeper truth of who we are with a renewed sense of what we value to give, and of stepping into our lives and into the world with courage and conviction.

We should aim not to be a person of success but rather to be a person of value. Being a person of value requires transcending self-absorption and taking a stand on the highest and holiest vision of life. It means doing more of what our deepest self desires. It means growing whole through crises.

Our purpose evolves as we grow, and crises have a unique way of accelerating that growth. Breakdowns often precede breakthroughs. Ironically, as things fall apart, we are forced to view our own lives more clearly; the scarier that times are, the more we can face our futures with courage. Life is short, fragile, and precious. Amid chaos lie new possibilities for growth.

Breakdowns often precede breakthroughs.

It's easy to become hypnotized by emotional contagion —the downside of crisis. But the stress associated with crisis can be a source of resilience. Research has consistently shown that people who persevere through war, natural disasters, economic strife, divorce, illness, and loss of loved ones can come out on the other side stronger and more resilient. The purpose question that crises often bring forth is: "What is life asking of me now?"

Purpose is not a luxury for the good times. In fact, it is even more essential for surviving and thriving in bad times. It is as old as humankind, no matter what adversity we face. Throughout human history, we have faced deep crises of spirit, forcing us to reckon with the age-old questions of why we live and how we live. To embrace those questions is the fundamental practice of aging on purpose.

The Practice of Aging on Purpose

Purpose is a verb; it is a path and a practice.

> Purpose *is a verb; it is a path and a practice.*

The idea is that any number of practices can help a person avoid or handle a late-life crisis, just so long as the person commits consistently to those practices.

For instance, the practice of journaling can help us better understand ourselves, but only if we journal on a regular basis. Engaging in real conversation with family and friends is a way of developing a better sense of what matters to us, but we have to actually have the conversations in order to achieve those insights. Writing a purpose statement gives us an aim, a compass to guide our actions in support of our deepest convictions. Unless we literally write down that purpose statement, however, our direction remains unclear.

The same goes for the practice of growing old on purpose. We have to do the things that enable us to do the thing we're trying to do. Once again, *purpose* is a verb. Having a purpose is great, but consistent practice is required.

Say we're interested in developing greater peace of mind through some sort of mindfulness practice like meditation, yoga, or tai chi. It won't happen unless we practice. Just thinking about meditation and wishing we would meditate more often doesn't bring the benefits of the practice. It's called a practice, after all, because you have to practice it.

The good news is that later life can be the perfect time to commit to such practices, since there are likely to be fewer obstacles in the way of our doing so. We're apt to no longer have the excuses, like a busy work schedule or a long daily commute, that enabled us to avoid committing ourselves earlier in our lives.

All of this is to make the obvious point that there's no time like the present. Sometimes, as we get older, we're inclined to think that it's too late to grow older—to get started doing something new—and besides, why not just relax and enjoy life as we know it?

Point taken.

On the other hand, our recognition that the time we have left is limited can be a spur to action. Knowing that we have limited years remaining to grow in some aspect of our life may be the inspiration to finally do so.

"Always Better"

Legendary dancer, choreographer, and wise elder Twyla Tharpe at age 79 shared her wisdom on aging in her 2019 book, *Keep It Moving: Lessons for the Rest of Your Life*: "I want to reprogram how you think about aging by getting rid of two corrosive ideas. First, that you need to emulate youth, resolving to live in a corner of the denial closet marked 'reserved for aged.' Second that your life must contract with time."

Another legendary and wise elder, Deborah Szekely, 98, takes those words to heart, eschewing the denial closet for center stage and expanding her life and horizons with each passing year. Since cofounding Rancho La Puerta, the world-renowned health spa in Tecate, Mexico, in 1940, Szekely has become an icon of the active and purposeful aging movement.

Her vitality and deep respect for the body's inherent wisdom are articulated in the spa's motto, *Siempre Mejor!* ("Always Better!"), which still guides her life and the work of the spa every day. "Nothing in my body is 98 years old, apart from my knowledge," she says. "Because the body largely renews itself every seven years, so very few things in me are older than that."

Her colleague Barry Shingle, director of guest relations and programming, who is half her age, says, "I can't fathom that Deborah is age 98! I've always feared and resisted aging. Deborah helped me over that. A person's soul or essence doesn't have an age. The light that shines in her eyes is not 98 years old."

Szekely embodies Rancho La Puerta's motto in her work with Shingle to create change and happiness for people. "Always Better!" has inspired her to become the poster child for purposeful aging.

She recommends that we rise every day with a sense of purpose in mind. "When I wake up, the first thing I do is take a pause. The computer and phone can wait. The first 20 minutes are a time to communicate with myself. I plan every day to be successful. And I choose to accept only positive thoughts—to look for the good in life. If I have a choice to make, I ask myself, 'Is it life-enhancing or life-diminishing?'"

She shares her perspective on purposeful aging: "Growing old means being purposeful—contributing to life. With elderhood comes the responsibility to share. I see aging as enrichment. Growing means you're never in the same place twice. You're always moving forward. Always better!

"I'm stimulated by nature. I'm seeing trees that I planted 75 years ago now as gigantic messengers. There are so many wise messages from trees; I see their strength, and that gives me strength." Just as Szekely's strength gives strength to all those associated with Rancho La Puerta. Always better!

"What Are Old People For?"

As Deborah Szekely illustrates, the term *old* has both objective and subjective meanings, a fixed and a relative sense, and descriptive and normative dimensions. It's a fraught term that evokes all sorts of reactions in all sorts of people at all sorts of times.

What is old, anyway? When does old begin? And who gets to say whether a person is old or not?

As we write this, Richard is 76; Dave is 63. Obviously, we're old. But in other senses we're not old at all. As we look back across the decades, the words of Bob Dylan in "My Back Pages" come to mind: "Ah, but I was so much older then, I'm younger than that now."

Spoiler alert: you're getting older; everyone alive is getting older. Eventually, if you live long enough, you'll be what is sometimes referred to as "old old." And yet, it's almost taboo to talk about getting old, much less acknowledge being old. Yet in spite of all the denial, most people want to live to be as old as possible.

Spoiler alert: you're getting older; everyone alive is getting older.

Always on the move, William H. Thomas, MD, author of *What Are Old People For?: How Elders Will Save the World*, is a man with a purpose: to challenge conventional views of aging. The *Wall Street Journal* has named him one of America's "top 10 innovators," and an entire chapter of the best seller *Being Mortal: Medicine and What Matters in the End*, by Atul Gawande, is devoted to Thomas, whom Gawande calls a "serial entrepreneur."

Far ahead of his time, "Dr. Bill," a Harvard Medical School–trained geriatrician, is particularly well known for pioneering the Eden Alternative, a radical system of humanizing nursing homes by introducing plants, pets, and even children into the environment. Now, he has given up practicing in favor of proselytizing about what it means to grow old.

In conversation with Richard, he says, "My view as a geriatrician is that we have to grow up twice—from childhood to adulthood and from adulthood to elderhood. If we don't mature during adolescence, all kinds of alarms go off. But for the second phase, there are no bells, beacons, alarms, or rituals if we miss it. I see aging as a strength, rich in developmental growth. What we need is a radical reimagining of longevity that makes elders central to our collective pursuit of happiness. How we perceive aging to a very large degree determines how we age. It's the story that matters. How people interpret their experience goes a long way to determining their well-being."

According to Thomas, our culture rewards the ideal of an older person who "still" does what they used to do. They fill their life with what has historically given them pleasure and fulfillment. They define success in backward-looking terms. The older person is admirable because they're still acting like a younger person.

But if "still" signifies success, then people who can't "still" do those younger things are failures. "This is wrong," contends Thomas. "We need to push the delete key on 'still.' In older adulthood, the word *still* is a sign of success; in childhood development, by contrast, the word *still* is a sign of failure."

As a geriatrician, Thomas believes that embracing death is a path to a more meaningful life. He has observed that "the happiest people are those who have chosen to shed the illusion of immortality. Knowing they have limited time, they focus more on purposeful relationships and less on pleasing others, less on stuff, more on experience. They choose to be their authentic selves."

Currently Thomas, on the cusp of elderhood himself, is focused on helping people of all ages to live in the place and manner of their choosing. "We're lucky if we get to grow old," he says. "I want to help people grow whole, not old."

Chapter Seven

Will I Earn a Passing Grade in Life?

One of the things we hear when we talk to people about aging on purpose is, "It's easy for you. You have your health and a steady income and a roof over your head. It's not so simple for people in more challenging circumstances. How can people explore purpose as they age when they're isolated and alone or with chronic illness or working multiple jobs just to make ends meet?"

Absolutely; we get it. As educated white males, we, Richard and Dave, are both fortunate and privileged. We've certainly had our challenges, but so far we've been lucky to have experienced neither major health problems nor significant economic setbacks in our lives. We do not doubt that our life experiences have influenced our perspective on growing old. The perspectives that both of us have on later life are surely due in part to the generally positive experience that each of us has had in our lives, as well as to our genes, our crucibles, and our choices.

We think there are several ways to respond to this issue—acknowledging all the while that we are incredibly lucky to be able to respond at all.

First—and this is not to downplay anyone's physical, economic, or emotional challenges—it bears noting that getting old isn't naturally easy for anyone. Yes, some people, for all sorts of reasons, many of which have nothing to do with them and everything to do with inequities and injustices endemic to contemporary society, have it tougher than others; but no one, no matter their gender, race, economic status, physical ability, or you name it, gets to avoid the inevitable questions that ensue as death approaches ever closer.

Second, for everyone, at some point (or points), life is going to be difficult; there's no getting around that. There is, however, getting beyond it, and that's what the path of aging on purpose is all about. Mindset, of course, is key. As everyone learned in Psychology 101, we can't control what happens, but we can control our reactions to what happens. Certainly, the harder the challenge, the harder this is to do. But one of the gifts of being old is having had lots of opportunities to practice doing so and to get better at managing our reactions to life's vicissitudes.

Third, even the most fortunate among us (and here we count ourselves) will, with each passing year, confront circumstances that challenge our conceptions of what it means to age purposefully. No matter how lucky we are, there will come times that are painful and difficult, and that require us to learn and grow from our experiences in order to give of our ourselves going forward. We recognize that in spite of our good fortune (or perhaps because of it), there will, for all of us, be a time for what Viktor Frankl, in the postscript to *Man's Search for Meaning*, calls "tragic optimism"—the case for saying yes to life despite the inevitable tragedies we all will experience.

Life can present us with extremely difficult challenges, and yes, we may feel defeated by those challenges, especially when we compare ourselves with others. But in the end—and the middle, too, for that matter—this life is all we have; and so, we may as well practice an attitude of tragic optimism.

Our aim in writing this book is to offer the path and practice of aging on purpose. In doing so, we aspire to share the tragic optimism that is our choice as we age.

For an illustration of that spirit and that choice, consider the following story.

Life was good: a great family, a leadership role in a successful company, a position in life and work that afforded numerous opportunities to make a real, positive difference in the world.

Then, bam! Everything changed.

For Ed Rapp, then group president of Caterpillar Inc., "life happened while he was busy making other plans" when he was diagnosed, at age 56, with amyotrophic lateral sclerosis (ALS), also known as Lou Gehrig's disease. Not surprisingly, he immediately retired from his position; somewhat surprisingly, he was completely transparent with others about his reason for doing so.

Extremely surprising, though, at least for Rapp, was the outpouring he received from colleagues and friends who came forth to offer their encouragement and support. Dozens of messages he received concluded with the admonition, "Stay strong!"

And staying strong is exactly what Rapp has done, having embraced a new challenge and become a leader in the global effort to research, treat, and find a cure for ALS.

Rapp's stated purpose for decades had been "to positively impact the people and responsibilities experienced through life." After his ALS diagnosis, his purpose never wavered. He founded Stay Strong vs. ALS, which as of the end of 2020 raised over $14 million for ALS research, a good portion of which came from the networks of colleagues and friends he built while at Caterpillar. He likens his ALS work to "building haystacks in the hope that research will find the needle."

At Caterpillar, Rapp recalls, they used to say, "The road to progress starts with a road." Rapp's road began on a farm in Pilot Grove, Missouri, where he graduated from high school in a class of 30 students. Small wonder that when he enrolled at the University of Missouri, he felt out of place and left behind. In response, he took a leadership class where he embraced a "daily prescription" of goal setting and purpose-based affirmations.

Today, he uses that same prescription, which drove his success at Caterpillar, to counsel ALS patients when they first learn of their heartbreaking prognosis: two to five years to live. Rapp draws upon his own experience in doing so. "The only times I cried," he admits, "was telling my kids and telling my parents." When his father-in-law expressed sorrow over Rapp's condition, lamenting that it was "such a sad story," Rapp responded, "If I can make a difference in ALS, it will have been a good life."

Rapp embodies Viktor Frankl's concept of tragic optimism, the choice to be the light in an otherwise dark tunnel. He observes that "many people who retire eventually want to engage in a life that makes a difference. But, they say, they just don't know how."

Rapp shows how by sharing his daily protocol to fight ALS: diet, exercise, and faith. Every night, after prayers, when he lays his head upon the pillow, he asks himself three questions: "Did I approach the day with the right mental attitude?" "Did I clearly demonstrate to my family that I'm all in on fighting ALS?" and "Did I in some small way make a difference in the broader fight against ALS?"

Every morning, when he rises, he reaffirms his purpose to positively impact people. His tragic optimism is the light that continues to illuminate that effort.

It's been said that "Life is the act of drawing without an eraser." For Rapp, even with ALS, the act of drawing continues. Against all odds, he is staying strong. As we write this, his gait is challenged and he walks with two arm crutches, but his strength and breathing capacity are good.

He says, "While my challenge is ALS, the disease has illuminated the fact that everyone in life deals with adversity in some size, shape, or form. As we all take on our challenges at hand, the good Lord won't measure us by events, announcements, job titles, personal challenges, or even a diagnosis. We will all be measured by how we respond and the contribution we make. *I just want to make a passing grade.*"

His humility is impressive; in the school of life, he surely deserves an A-plus.

So, how do we, like Ed Rapp, earn a passing grade in the school of life?

It begins with a yearning, a yearning that we find articulated in the poetry of the great 13th-century Sufi mystic poet Rumi. Somehow, Rumi has given voice to an unconscious yearning in the Western psyche.

Could it be that this yearning is for a passing grade? A yearning for purpose?

"What have you bought with your life?" he asks us in one of his poem's titles. "Through what work have you reached your life's end?"

Across the centuries, Rumi's voice calls to us and reminds us of why we were born. This very idea is perhaps best captured in his simple, beautiful line, "What you seek is seeking you."

Here, Rumi is reminding us that we all, like Ed Rapp, have a purpose in life, one that is actually seeking us. "What is life asking of me now?" The answer is what our purpose is, regardless of the adversities we face.

In other words, it's imperative to listen to our inner voice, knowing that what calls to us calls for a reason. Or, as Rumi puts it, "Everyone has been made for some particular work, and the desire for that work has been put into every heart."

> "Everyone has been made for some particular work, and the desire for that work has been put into every heart."

Life often moves so fast that we fail to take time to live with the questions whose answers make life meaningful. Rumi awakens us to such questions time and again: "What is real connection between people?" "What is any of us but a straw in a storm?" "Why this inconsistency, that we live within love, yet run away?" Though they arise from more than 800 years ago, his questions remain relevant and probing for our lives today.

Time and again, Rumi assures us that mattering matters, that we matter, that we're not accidental, that we have a reason for being, and that the most important task in our lives is to listen for the "call" and to earn a passing grade in life by answering it.

In Rumi's words from "Fihi Ma Fihi #4," translated by Kabir Helminski in *The Rumi Collection* (2000): "There is one thing in the world that should not be forgotten. You may forget everything except that one thing, without there being any cause for concern. If you remember everything else, but forget that one thing, you will have accomplished nothing. It would be as if a king sent you to a village on a specific mission. If you went and performed a hundred other tasks, but neglected the task for which you were sent, it would be as though you had done nothing. The human being therefore has come into the world for a specific purpose and aim. If one does not fulfill that purpose, one has done nothing."

Instead of speaking to the followers of any one faith, Rumi's words inspire faith in the divine independent of a particular perspective on God. His voice transcends age, time, gender, ethnicity, and religious or spiritual background. "The lamps are different / But the Light is the same," he writes in "One, One, One," "One matter, one energy, one Light, one Light-mind / Endlessly emanating all things."

Rumi's consistent engagement with the very questions that animate religion, philosophy, psychology, art, and other fundamental human activities provides us with insights into our own deepest questions about what we are called to do in life. His answers, so simple, so eloquent, speak to us timelessly; from his poem by the same title, "Let the beauty we love be what we do."

Those words could be signposts on the path of purposeful aging: Let the beauty of what we love be what we do in later life.

Crossing the threshold from adulthood to elderhood is about that activity. As Richard puts it, "It's about claiming my voice and my right and responsibility to show up, to speak. It means waking up every single day, grateful to be alive and to be growing and giving. It means living with the intention to earn a passing grade."

Growing whole is spiritual work. It is work that acknowledges, yet transcends, the day-to-day challenges of aging and forges a connection to something bigger than our own individual cares and concerns—something that helps us to feel rooted in the ongoing, universal, ancient, and enduring story, in which we each play our essential role.

The Sage-ing Way of Age-ing

Nearly all of us, at one time or another, have met an older person and thought, "That's who I want to be like when I grow old!" Perhaps it's even a fictional character who inspires us, like the feisty old lady Maude in the classic film comedy *Harold and Maude*, or the wise wizard Albus Dumbledore in the *Harry Potter* series. No matter what the source, though, the question remains: "Who do I want to be when I grow old?"

> *We have to work on ourselves today so as to grow into the old person we want to become tomorrow.*

Growth doesn't happen automatically with age, and we can't simply order the character traits online; we have to work at it. We have to work on ourselves today so as to grow into the old person we want to become tomorrow.

But how? Enter the sage.

The late Rabbi Zalman Schachter-Shalomi (better known as Reb Zalman), founder of the Spiritual Eldering Institute, was an advocate for a new approach to aging that he termed "sage-ing." In his best seller *From Age-ing to Sage-ing: A Profound New Vision of Growing Older* (1997), he writes, "An elder is a person who is still growing, still a learner, still with potential and whose life continues to have within it promise for, and connections to, the future. An elder is still in pursuit of happiness, joy, and pleasure, and his birthright to these remains intact. Moreover, an elder is a person who deserves respect and honor and whose work is to synthesize wisdom from long life experience and formulate this into a legacy for future generations."

Reb Zalman's belief in the universality of spiritual truth led him to study with Sufi masters, Buddhist teachers, Native American elders, Catholic monks, and humanistic and transpersonal psychologists. His work became the Sage-ing International organization. This sage-ing view is of aging as a spiritual practice that sees everyday service as the natural result of continued inner growth.

So, who is a "sage"? Reb Zalman taught that a sage is a work in progress—a seeker and a lifelong learner. To sage is to age purposefully—to make purposeful choices and take responsible action. Sages are known not just for what they do but also for how they do it: with compassion, respect, integrity, and joy. The process of becoming a sage takes time and requires us to examine our feelings and choices in order to earn life's passing grade.

The psychologist Erik Erikson coined the term *generativity*, which refers to the need felt by elders to nurture and guide young people and to contribute to the success of the next generation. Generativity, he argued, is not only good for society but also good for individuals. At the generative stage of life, we have a wealth of life experiences and, hopefully, some wisdom gained from many life lessons along the way. Sage-ing is generativity in action, as we draw upon those lessons to recognize our unique legacy and share it for the benefit of those who follow us chronologically.

Given the benefits of generativity, it behooves us to step onto the purpose path. One way to do so is to visualize going through a typical day as a generative elder, a sage. Picture yourself waking up with a sense of purpose and going to bed fulfilled, having made a significant difference in at least one young person's life that very day. Imagine feeling relevant. How can you begin to make the image a reality right now?

By walking the purpose path, we add aliveness—and perhaps extra years—to our lives. And not just more years to our lives; we also add more life to our years!

In his wonderful 2014 *New Yorker* essay "This Old Man: Life in the Nineties," Roger Angell, age 93 at the time, writes with passion and humor about the pleasures associated with friends inviting him out to dinner or someone leaving a roasted chicken on his doorstep. He reflects on the "palpable joy" he feels, even at age 93, when watching baseball, or reading poetry, or listening to Mozart horn concertos. "Getting old," he says, "is the second-biggest surprise of my life, but the first, by a mile, is our unceasing need for deep attachment and intimate love."

Love makes the world go round—we know it when we're 19 or 30, but no less so when we're 93. The passions we feel as young people still burn within us as old people—perhaps less hot but no less brightly. And keeping those passions burning, through deep attachments and intimate love, is what helps us to earn a passing grade in life.

Chapter Eight

How Can I Grow Whole as I Grow Old?

We talk a lot in this book about "growing whole" as we grow old. But how does that connect to how people really feel about growing older?

In fact, growing whole is, at its core, a feeling. Like love, it's best understood by experience.

To grow whole means, above all, to truly become the person you authentically are. It means accepting and embracing your thoughts, your feelings, your hopes and dreams, your fears and anxieties—all the desirable and undesirable parts of your being.

Growing whole is about integrity and integration. Integrity can be defined as keeping the small promises you make to yourself and others. It requires saying what you mean and meaning what you say; ultimately, it's about speaking the truth—especially the truth about yourself. It involves bringing into balance all parts of our person—our mind, our body, our soul or spirit, everything that contributes to our sense of who we are—and doing so in a manner that allows us to live life with curiosity, choice, and courage.

One of the best things about growing old is that we don't have to default anymore to being someone or something we're not. To grow whole means that we can bring to the world the wholeness of our being, without pretense. This can be uncomfortable, particularly if it means we recognize aspects of ourselves that are less than ideal. Giving sunlight to these shortcomings, though, and integrating them into a more complete picture of the person we aspire to be allows us to achieve a greater sense of wholeness—a more complete expression of all that we are.

Growing whole doesn't happen all at once, and there's no end point at which we can say that wholeness has been achieved. In fact, it's way more about the growing than the whole.

One way we can tell if we're growing whole is that we feel less fear. This doesn't mean that we're never anxious or afraid; it means we're less fearful about showing the world who we really are. We're more willing to present ourselves, warts and all, for others to see, and far less fearful about admitting

One way we can tell if we're growing whole is that we feel less fear.

when we're wrong, or if we made a mistake, or that we have room to grow and improve.

Ultimately, growing whole is about growing more compassionate—not just toward others but toward ourselves as well. Doctor Suess's famous Grinch grew more whole when his heart grew three sizes in one day; we grow in wholeness every time we listen better, learn better, or love better.

> *. . . we grow in wholeness every time we listen better, learn better, or love better.*

It's ironic, but also poignant and promising, that as we age and our bodies fall increasingly subject to entropy, we are able to counteract that physical reality with the emotional and spiritual work of becoming more compassionate, as our mind, heart, and spirit come together in harmony.

The Great Midlife Edit

In his 2018 best seller *Wisdom @ Work: The Making of a Modern Elder*, Chip Conley liberated the term *elder* from the ageist stigma of *elderly* and inspired readers to embrace wisdom as the path to growing whole.

In conversation with Richard about his work, he says, "A new kind of elder is emerging—not the elder of the past treated with reverence, but the elder of today valued for their relevance. To be relevant, we need to grow whole. Growing whole is about integrity, and that means bringing all of who you are at any time, to any place, with anyone you're with. When I'm with someone who is 'whole,' I feel that deep well of soulful wisdom, not ego. The person is not packaging him- or herself to look good or impress me."

Growing whole requires creating a new synthesis of who we are and what we have to offer the world. Growing whole requires shifting our focus from "What's in it for me?" to "How may I serve?"

Conley asserts that "the good life is a generative life, a giving life. My former default life was being a successful 'doer'—'the little engine that could'! In fact, we used to give that book to all of my employees. The one indicator of our (and their) success was our 'can do' attitude.

"Now, my primary operating system is soul, not ego. I'm moved from 'can do' to 'conduit.' As a modern elder conduit, I'm channeling my energy and gifts for the common good. I'm not striving anymore; I'm flowing and hopefully supporting others on their path."

Modern elders are also "menterns," which is Conley's term for "mutual mentorship," a life full of reciprocity. He says, "Being in a mentern relationship is like being in a dance where there's a natural rhythm you get into without being self-conscious about your moves. Sometimes you're leading; sometimes they're leading."

Modern elders are as curious as they are wise. Conley's curiosity, and his background as a boutique hotelier, called him to cofound the Modern Elder Academy in El Pescadero on Mexico's Baja Peninsula—a place that helps people navigate their midlife transitions. As the world's first "midlife wisdom school," the Academy offers programs to help people "reset, restore, and repurpose their lives." It's a place where wisdom is not taught but shared.

Conley explains that the "compadres" (as Modern Elder Academy students are called) are people who realize that it is time for their "great midlife edit." The first half of their lives was often defined by the question "What does the world expect of me?" The midlife edit question becomes "How can I serve the world while also seeking contentment?" Like Conley, they come to see their operating system in the second half of life shift from ego to soul. "So, to age purposefully," says Conley, "we must become great editors. The second half of life is more about attuning than attaining."

Aging on Purpose as Growing Whole

Writing this book has been for us an exercise in attuning. It has asked that we honestly confront the reality of our own aging and dying. It has required that we face our fears about growing old and try to write about them personally and from the heart.

"I'm not fearful about aging," admits Richard, "I'm fearful about suffering. I'm also fearful about something happening to my wife, Sally, or to my children, Andrew and Greta, or to their families, or to my close friends. There's also now the fear about whether I'll be ready to end it peacefully when the end comes. I'm hopeful that

I'll be able to deal with my final days consciously; the prospect of failing to do that, however, is frightening."

The process of writing this book has, like the process of growing older, pushed us into uncharted territory, where we no longer have answers and where what has gotten us here successfully may not be what we need going forward.

For more than four decades, Richard has provided guidance and direction to others seeking a sense of purpose and calling in their lives. "Now, it's time for me to undertake a new quest to live in this question: 'What is life asking of me now?' My focus is slowly shifting from achievement to living from the heart, from a wider audience to deeper relationships. I still honor my old life for all that it has done for me; it's gotten me this far. But in order to grow whole, I need to let go."

The Indian poet and philosopher Rabindranath Tagore wrote in *Gitanjali* (1910), "When old words die out on the tongue, new melodies break forth from the heart; and where the old tracks are lost, new country is revealed with its wonders."

Later life can be a time filled with wonder, but, as Tagore points out, that requires getting off the beaten track. It means not playing the same old song, but rather allowing new melodies to break forth. How can we tell if we're not just repeating the same tired tunes? How can we find the courage to forge our own new path?

A sincere commitment to growing whole may help, along with an appetite for intensity—an idea that may sound counter to the common conception of old age, but that poet, playwright, and suffragist Florida Scott-Maxwell articulated clearly when she was in her 80s: "Age puzzles me. I thought it was a quiet time . . . I grow more intense as I age."

That intensity is most manifest in the relationships in our lives. The older we get, the closer we draw toward death, the more important those relationships become. And paradoxically, the deeper those relationships, the further from death we feel. Do meaningful relationships lead to aliveness, good health, and well-being, or vice versa? In all likelihood, it goes both ways.

Do You Want to Live to 120?

How long can the appetite for intensity last? The May 2013 issue of *National Geographic* featured four different infants on four alternate covers with the headline, "This Baby Will Live to Be 120," and a footnote: "It's not hype. New science could lead to very long lives."

Being more than halfway there, we asked ourselves, "Do we want to live to be 120? Is that really something to aim for?"

The answer to that question surely changes depending on a person's stage in life. When Dave was in his 40s, he routinely claimed that he wanted to live to be 112; now, in his 60s, 85 strikes him as plenty. Richard has consistently thought that 95 was his number; now, in his 70s, that's still his aim.

Most people are fascinated by and long for longevity, but at the same time they are unenthusiastic about and resistant to aging. To paraphrase television commentator Andy Rooney (who died at 92), there's something paradoxical that the idea of living a long life appeals to nearly everyone, but the idea of getting old doesn't appeal to anyone.

Do you mind getting older? What most of us really want is to live a long and healthy life, what is affectionally referred to as a "ripe old age." Ripening means becoming fully developed; it suggests a sweetness that combines quality of life with number of years. But just as a fruit ripens only under the right conditions and care, our hope of making it to a ripe old age (although not necessarily 120) will be realized only through some purposeful choices.

Ripening in nature is, of course, essentially a vehicle for regeneration. The seeds of the ripened fruit or vegetable are sown for the next generation to emerge. In our ripe old age, we look for ways to contribute to the ongoing regeneration of humanity. In later life, it's obviously not about having children—those days, if they ever were, are long past. Now, it's about sharing one's passions, talents, and gifts with the world on purpose.

A Life Portfolio

The old-old people, age 80-plus, are the world's fastest-growing demographic; the number of people in the United States aged 100 or more leaped 44 percent from 2000 to 2014. What's going on? Is it something in the water?

According to Dan Buettner, explorer, National Geographic Fellow, best-selling author, and founder of the Blue Zones Project, it's more about choice. "We can live a shorter life with more years of disability, or we can live the longest possible life with the fewest bad years. The centenarians showed me that the choice is largely up to us."

Buettner discovered five places in the world—dubbed Blue Zones—where people tend to live the longest, healthiest lives. In these zones, people live much longer than average—frequently hitting the century mark—and often avoid age-related conditions, notably dementia.

"Blue Zones residents," he explains, "move constantly through each day, live with purpose, and do it all with a little help from their friends."

Buettner has adopted those principles in his own life. "My next expedition is the art of life—a journey of discovering how to act my agelessness. I think adulthood is overrated. It's fun to act like a kid; it keeps me young! I hold three distance cycling records in the Guinness book, and I still get great pleasure from riding my bike everywhere."

Happiness, it turns out, is key to longevity. "I like thinking about happiness," says Buettner, "in the same way you think of your financial portfolio. You want it balanced—for the short term and the long term. My Life Portfolio balances purpose, pleasure, and pride. A good life, for me, is one that reprioritizes those three essentials.

"To live the good life, as you say, we need to unpack, to let go of things that no longer serve your purpose. The major let-go for me is people. When someone shows me their true colors and those colors are toxic, I don't go back. I'm more attracted to people now with moral integrity."

According to the Harvard Study of Adult Development, close relationships figure more in keeping people happy throughout their life than IQ, genes, social class, or any other single factor. The study's research shows that people who were most satisfied with their relationships at age 50 are the healthiest at age 80.

Buettner, at age 60, says, "I'm a test case for that study. I feel like I'm on a happiness upswing because of my healthy relationships with my significant other, family, and grandkids."

Having what Blue Zones calls a "right outlook" on life makes a huge difference, and self-reflection is an important part of this. Buettner thanks Richard for giving him some tools for this. "I learned from Richard how to do a self-inventory—a purpose checkup—and I find it easier now to be satisfied with the reality of my life—the simple things. I spent a lifetime chasing cool mysteries and traveled to the ends of the earth. My purpose is still to 'find the traditional peoples, distilling their wisdom and repacking the lessons learned in ways that are relevant to people today."

Most people are aware that their chances of living to an old-old age increase with regular exercise and enhanced physical fitness. But what about the magic longevity pill of purpose? To age well also requires that we exercise our sense of purpose. And that means growing socially and spiritually, both components of an overall sense of purposeful aging that improves our chances of living a long and healthy life.

As Dan Buettner observes, purposeful aging does not happen automatically. Biomedical interventions can enable us to add years to our life; what sorts of interventions will enable us to meet the challenge of adding life to our years?

Chapter Nine

How Will My Music Play On?

There's no shortage of advice these days about aging; most of it, though, is focused on antiaging—how to deny and distance what happens as we grow old. Not so for Parker Palmer. The best-selling author, teacher, and activist is intentionally growing whole. In word and deed, he celebrates the gifts that accrue to us in later life.

"At age 81," says Palmer, "I'm truly on the brink of everything. The older I've gotten, the harder it becomes not to think of my mortality. While I'm in decent health, and as sound of mind as I've ever been—a low bar—it's time to clear the way for whatever's next."

He is surprised by how much he enjoys being old. Drawing on eight decades of life and work, he embraces the questions that age raises and the answers it provides.

Echoing the lyrics of the Janis Joplin hit "Me and Bobby McGee," he muses, "Old is just another word for nothing left to lose. Above all, I like being old because the view from the brink is a panorama of my life. It awakens me to new perspectives of my past, present, and, yes, future."

In the last few years, Palmer "retired" from his long-time work as a teacher to focus on his family, his writing, and a new project called the Growing Edge that he started with a younger colleague, singer-songwriter Carrie New-comer. "I can't imagine life without a sense of vocation. So, I keep stretching myself vocationally." To that end, he recently collaborated with Newcomer on a series of songs to accompany his most recent book, *On the Brink of Every-thing: Grace, Gravity, and Getting Old,* as well as an original song, "The Music Will Play On," which encapsulates his attitude toward aging and his commitment to, as he puts it, "use what I know for the greater good."

About a decade ago, inspired by practices within his Quaker faith, Palmer held a series of in-depth dis-cernment practices—what are known among Friends communities as a "Clearness Committee"—to explore his own aging. He sought insight into two questions related to growing old: "What do I need to let go of?" and "What do I need to hang on to?" The discussions led to a major breakthrough: "'Hang on to' is a scarcity model. The real question became, 'What do I want to give myself to?' That's an abundance model."

This bias toward an abundance model is reflected in one of Palmer's longstanding messages—one that becomes clearer in later years—that the difficulties we face on our path through life are the path itself. They are not detours but rather opportunities to awaken and to serve. The key to a meaningful life is not to change our life but to choose it—to intentionally see whatever is happening as our chosen path. By doing this, we are taking the first steps toward what it means to "let your life speak," the title of Palmer's classic best seller.

"Before I can tell my life what I want to do with it, I must listen to my life telling me who I am," he says. "As we age, it's important to get clear about the difference between the job we make a living at and the vocation by which we make meaning." Nearly all of us will stop doing that job in later life, but we can still follow our vocation and make meaning until the very end.

Palmer lives by the words of St. Benedict: "Keep death daily before your eyes." No matter how rich, famous, powerful, or healthy you are, death is coming. "So, I'm not going to wax poetic about aging and dying. I simply know that the first is a privilege and the second is not up for negotiation. It's a blessed thing simply to be one of those who've lived long enough to say, 'I'm getting old.'"

"Keep death daily before your eyes."

Palmer reflects that he cannot imagine a sadder way to die than feeling you had never shown up in the world authentically as yourself. "But if you can say you showed up more often than not, 'the music will play on' and you can die happy. You will have become what you were meant to be."

> "But if you can say you showed up more often than not, 'the music will play on' and you can die happy."

Eventually, we all need to be willing to face the deepest, darkest secrets we harbor about ourselves. Genuine happiness turns on the courage to acknowledge the painful aspects of life alongside the pleasurable ones. An integral component of a good life is an openness to experiences that aren't typically considered good. Depression, for example, cannot be denied. The compassion and loving-kindness that evolved from Palmer's three major bouts of depression have led him to an even greater sense of equanimity. Ultimately, he says, "I'm just glad for every day of life!"

"I have fears," he admits, "always have, always will. But as time lengthens behind me like a shadow, and the time ahead dwindles, my feeling is gratitude for the gift of life. How we travel between birth and death is ours to choose. Knowing ourselves and sinking our roots into the ground of our being is critical in old age."

The desire to sink those roots has made Palmer a huge believer in the power and necessity of silence and solitude. He journeys each year to places like the Boundary Waters Canoe Area Wilderness in Minnesota and the mountains around Santa Fe, New Mexico, in search of quiet and calm. "Becoming comfortable with solitude and silence can ease the transition from life to death—a journey we must make alone back into the silence from which we came."

Dying Young as Old as Possible

As Jim Morrison of the rock group the Doors sang, "No one here gets out alive."

But that's a good thing. The aspirations of billionaires investing millions of dollars in the effort to cheat death to the contrary, the prospect of dying cannot be avoided. Part of what gives life meaning is its ephemeral nature. If we lived forever, much of the sweetness of life would be lost. Special occasions like births, marriages, and graduations would no longer be so special, since they'd be just another event in an endless line of repeated experiences.

Of course, we all know it intellectually: as soon as we're born, we start dying; it's only a matter of time until we meet our maker. But emotionally, we keep that knowledge at bay. Most of us live in denial about the reality of death; perversely, we imagine it to be something that happens to everyone else but not us.

In order to live as fully as possible, though, especially in later life, we have to come to terms with dying. We have to accept our inevitable demise and make choices accordingly.

Most people want to die young as old as possible. The way to do so is to live each day knowing it could be your last, but with the hope that your efforts will carry on long after you're gone.

This all sounds great and is no doubt easier said than done, but what does it look like in real life as we age, with all of its attendant losses, aches and pains, and general decline? That's up to each of us as we confront every new day. One thing is for certain, though, and applies to us all: we're only as alive as we're living *for* something. Unless we have a reason to get out of bed—even if it's something as simple as to pull some weeds in our garden or feed our cat—we may as well just pull the covers over our head and stay there.

We all have pain. We all suffer. And we all will die. This is the natural order of things. The widespread desire for a "good death" is perhaps better understood as a proxy desire for having lived well. Ultimately, how we lived is far more important than how we die. Our sense of meaning has little to do with how long we lived or what happens at the moment we expire, but rather has everything to do with whether the way we live is aligned with our perceived purpose.

There are those who question whether life can be meaningful given the certainty that we will die. Yet, it's the very awareness that life is ephemeral that makes meaning possible. Understanding this is one of the true gifts of aging. A deeper appreciation for the transitory nature of life can motivate us to prioritize what really matters. Because mattering matters.

End in Mind

"How do you want to die?" is a question that few are willing to ask and even fewer are willing to answer.

Not so for Emmy Award–winning journalist, radio and television personality, and author Cathy Wurzer. As founder of the End in Mind Project, a website and community effort to ignite fearless conversations into the subject of dying, Wurzer is passionate about exploring how our attitudes toward death inform our experience of living. Her purpose these days is to help others live fully—with integrity, meaning, and joy—no matter how long they have left to live.

The End in Mind Project is based on a series of broadcast conversations she had with Bruce Kramer, a professor and academic dean who faced his final days of living with ALS head-on, by choosing to be at peace with his inevitable demise rather than being consumed with anxiety and despair. His example taught Wurzer to look at death not as an end but rather as a "transition into something else, just another life transition."

Kramer's courage inspired her to help people start living with their own end in mind. This isn't just focusing on dying, though—"It's about the living," says Wurzer, "fully living our lives right to the end."

Engaging in real conversations about death, Wurzer helps people achieve a level of comfort with the uncomfortable. She says she wants to be a "catalyst for cultural change," leading people to an acceptance of what, along with birth, is the most normal event in all our lives—the end of it.

As a regional celebrity on public radio and television, Wurzer has the ability to draw people into an examination of their lives at every age and every stage by asking, "What does it mean to live with the end in mind?" As Bruce Kramer approached his own end, he instructed Wurzer to "look for the ripples in our work." When she asked how, he answered, "Don't worry; you'll know it when you see it." And then he added, "I want you to be with me all the way."

"End in mind is not a checkpoint or a milestone," she says, "it's a mindset." She, like Parker Palmer, quotes the Benedictine wisdom "Keep death daily before your eyes" as her inspiration for that mindset.

Wurzer recognizes that fear is a normal human reaction to the knowledge that our lives will eventually come to an end. Yet, if we can find a sense of peace alongside that fear, we can learn to live with gratitude for the time we've had and the time we have left.

Gratitude is good for us. Research has shown that it is consistently associated with greater happiness, better health, and a stronger ability to deal with the tough stuff of life. Wurzer shares her gratitude practice: "I have a 'gratitude jar' at home where each day, I'll write something down that I'm thankful for. There's a little pile of paper slips in that old blue glass Ball jar.

Gratitude is good for us.

Gratitude helps connect me to something larger than my puny self, whether that's to other humans, nature, or God. It guides me to appreciating life's preciousness."

Through the End in Mind Project, Wurzer has gathered together an impressive array of scholars and practitioners in the field of well-being to delve more deeply into issues of death and dying. She is transforming a conversation no one wants to have into a real one of deep engagement and gratitude for the gift of life.

She claims to be the "queen of busyness." "In my line of work, we're rewarded for being in motion. But my busyness is really a deflection of stuff I still need to work on. My goal is to die with joy—to look forward to the next plane of existence with gratitude." She is on the path of purposeful aging with the end in mind.

Making Friends with Death

Death starts sending us text messages when we're in our late 20s or early 30s.

We get our first gray hair or that first crow's foot, or we notice that we're not recovering from a night on the town as quickly as we used to.

That's Death out there, reminding us that he's just waiting patiently for now but keeping an eye on us all the time.

In our 40s and 50s, the messages get more frequent. Death is like one of those national political organizations you've somehow subscribed to that inundate your email in-box with updates almost daily. Back pain, baldness, erectile dysfunction, menopause: that's Death, keeping us apprised of his attention, letting us know that he hasn't forgotten about us and looks forward to getting to know us better in the not-too-distant future.

In our 60s and beyond, most of us have had a number of personal encounters with Death. He's come for our parents, colleagues, friends, and partners, and even, in some tragic cases, our children. We don't need his reminders anymore, but he continues to stay in touch with special delivery packages like high blood pressure, heart disease, bone density loss, and cancer diagnoses.

You've really got to hand it to Death—he's in the background at every birthday, anniversary, and major event in later life. He never fails to eventually show up for all of us, regardless of race, creed, color, gender, sexual orientation, you name it. Death is the world's unparalleled expert in diversity, equity, and inclusion; ultimately, no one gets special consideration at his hands. Rich, poor, white, Black, male, female, citizen, immigrant, and so on—everyone, in the end, gets treated the same by Death's final embrace.

Consequently, it's strange that few of us make better friends with Death. You'd think that with all the attention he pays to each of us, more of us would make an effort to come to friendly terms with him. Instead of answering his messages and responding to his visits, though, we typically shun Death at every opportunity. He's the estranged family member we do our utmost to ignore, the childhood friend whose letters we never respond to, the next-door neighbor we can't be bothered to even say "hi" to.

And this is a shame, because by making friends with Death, we have the potential to make his inevitable visit to us go somewhat more smoothly. Getting to know Death, allowing Death into our lives and homes, even just a bit, means that when he finally comes in to take full possession, we'll be that much more prepared to turn it all over.

Easier said than done, of course, and often, even with the best of intentions, not done after all. But keeping that in mind, it behooves us to develop a better relationship with Death during the time we're alive—learning to live with Death, in other words, while we're still living with ourselves.

The Ultimate Conversation

Our reflections on death and dying bring us full circle, back to where we started: to our long conversation about growing old. Eventually, on that rainy afternoon in Minneapolis, we gave up on the Twins game and headed back to our respective homes.

But what we didn't give up on was the conversation— the long conversation that defines our old friendship. We continued wondering, as we have for the past three decades, what makes life worth living and how, as we age, can we retain a sense of purpose and vitality in our lives? How do we stay on the path of purposeful aging together?

Richard's stated purpose, "to grow and to give," provides a framework and determined the structure for this book. Those two aims—growing and giving—came to define a process by which we can continue to grow whole as we grow old.

It's a process that involves looking back over our life in order to grow and looking forward toward our death in order to keep giving as we age. In short, it's really about staying alive for as long as we live.

We realize that we're all going to die; along with birth, it's one of two realities in life that everyone shares. In spite (or perhaps because) of this, death is mysterious, troubling, and frightening.

The inevitability of death may make life seem meaningless. As we've wondered earlier, if we all end up dead, what's the purpose of living, anyway? Without death, though, how could life be meaningful at all? That life and death are inextricably linked is what makes our time here so poignant and precious. Life is simply too short to hold on or hold back.

By facing death, we can develop a *why* for living. By confronting the reality of our own dying, we can recommit to life with less fear. Admittedly, this is perhaps life's greatest challenge. Merely making it through the day-to-day, dealing with loss, suffering, setbacks, and decline, may be all one can do. Nevertheless, facing death squarely can enable us to clarify our sense of purpose and thus, paradoxically, feel more alive.

Three Ultimate Questions

An honest discussion about death is perhaps the most important conversation of all—we call it the Ultimate Conversation. There are no doubt as many ways to have this conversation as there are people to have it. We have found, though, that three big questions can be remarkably effective in fostering the Ultimate Conversation:

- ❖ What do you think happens when you die?

- ❖ How would you like to die?

- ❖ What gifts do you want to leave the world before you die?

As friends and coauthors, we, Richard and Dave, committed to having the Ultimate Conversation as a way to end this book. We reflected on the three questions about death and did our best to answer them honestly and forthrightly. In doing so, we learned much about each other, but even more about ourselves.

We encourage you to have an Ultimate Conversation of your own with friends or family members. Doing so really can be a matter of life or death.

Our Answers

....

What do you think happens when you die?

Richard: The idea of reincarnation has always fascinated me. Not the idea of dying and then coming back—a butterfly in the next life, for instance. But the idea of the cycles of life. I believe that a loving Creator created me (and you) to "grow and give" in a mysterious world. My next life might be revealed to me by our Creator . . . but probably not.

Gandhi once said, "All life is one." He might have said it to unite a spiritually diverse world, but I subscribe to that view literally. When my body goes, when my thought ceases, the "All" remains. I'm part of the "All" of life, and life will continue, so I will too, in some new, mysterious form.

Dave: I mostly agree with Richard, but I'm a little more skeptical about an ongoing experience after death. When I die, I think "I" cease to be. This container that houses my ego-shape, my *ahamkara*, as they put it in Vedic philosophy, dies, and the focused consciousness that "I" am disperses into the Universal Consciousness that exists in and behind all of reality. I like the metaphor of my "cup" of water—this life's consciousness—being tossed back into the ocean of consciousness. What made me me is still there, but it's so diluted that it's not possible that I would have any conception of "I"-ness. I believe the experience after death will be just like it was before birth—nothingness. And I'm OK with that; I was perfectly "happy" before I was born; I'll be similarly content after I'm dead.

How would you like to die?

Dave: Quickly, painlessly, and not in a hospital, if possible. I don't need to have all my friends and family around. I don't believe that it's tragic to die alone; I believe we all die alone, anyway. I don't crave some deathbed scene; just let me go off into a corner like a cat and die in peace. I realize, of course, that this is all wishful thinking. No one can predict what their last days will be like, and it's unrealistic of me to imagine that I know now what I'll want when I get there. Mainly, I want some degree of autonomy and agency. I'm the one who's going to be doing the dying; as much as possible, therefore, I'd like to die in my own way, on my own terms.

Richard: Viktor Frankl's insight that enduring suffering could provide purpose in life was a major eye-opener for me. Bearing suffering with grace and courage might be a purpose in itself. That said, I don't want to die; but more clearly, I don't want to suffer. Will I still be writing a decade from now? I hope so, but who can say? What I do know is that I'm already looking forward to another book!

Sure, I could get charged by a young bull elephant in the bush in Tanzania, then buried right there, under a baobab tree. That's a scenario I could live—that is, die—with. But, a more likely scenario that I prefer is to die sitting up and appreciating small pleasures like seeing a favorite bird outside our window while sharing a nice glass of red wine and exchanging hugs with my wife, Sally. These small pleasures will be enough to feed my soul up to my last breath.

What gifts do you want to leave the world before you die?

Richard: What survives me is my impact on others—one person at a time, one day at a time, every day of my life. My gift is simply to make a positive difference in one person's life, every day. When I die, I hope that my epitaph will read, "Always on purpose."

Dave: I'd like, above all, to give the gift of kindness wherever I go. This doesn't mean—as I'm sure my family, friends, and colleagues would attest to—that I'm always the nicest, kindest person around. But I would like my ongoing offer to the world to be that of someone who cares about others; who is thoughtful and open to new perspectives; who is willing to admit when he is wrong; who is loyal, dependable, and funny; and who tries to make the experience of living a little bit better for everyone. Above all, I should like my gift to the world to be my gratitude for the world's endless gifts to me.

Our own Ultimate Conversation has turned out to be an impetus for deeper reflections and has helped us see more clearly how death can teach us about the path of purposeful aging. We've come to understand better how purpose is a fundamental motivating force for all humanity. It brings a wholeness to who we are, a sense of meaning to what we do, and a deeper connection to the world around us.

Afterword

....

Staying on the Path

Having read through this book, you may be asking yourself, *What do I do now? How do I step onto (or stay on) the path of purposeful aging?*

The honest answer is that there is no one way, no one-size-fits-all approach. The path for each of us is unique. Society used to guide us down a default path of life, from birth to school, work, retirement, and death. But no more. These days, we must design our own path and take charge of our future, no matter what our age or stage of life.

In order to age well, we need to unpack our past, repack for the future, and repeat. We need to make growing old our central life task. This is why the path of purposeful aging requires a practice. It's things we do consistently, with mindfulness and purpose, that enable us to follow our own path.

As a way to get started on (or continue with) that path, we invite you to revisit the book and engage in the following practice: Approach the book as you would if it were a personal journal. Read it slowly, a little bit at a time. Reflect on the themes that speak to you. Interact with what you read. Write your own thoughts in a *Purposeful Aging Journal* that you create as you reread the book.

For example, which chapter do you find most important at this time in your life? Write your thoughts and reflections about it in your journal.

Read the chapter title/question for each chapter as if it has your name on it. If it engages you, work it through in your journal.

Consider reading the book together with a "purpose partner"—someone who is as curious to age purposefully as you are. Talk about your feelings as you read certain sections aloud to each other.

If you have a number of friends or acquaintances who intend to grow whole, set up a study group that meets every couple of weeks, taking one chapter at a time. This book is an excellent tool for group discussion and discovery—at home, in community, or in a faith organization.

Consider the questions that frame each chapter as ways to explore the path of purposeful aging. What follows are merely suggestions, not directions. Consider them a guide, rather than guidelines. Ultimately, the path of purposeful aging is a path you choose yourself.

Chapter One: *Old? Who, Me?*

Describe the finest chapter in your life thus far. What made it the finest? How can you manifest those qualities in the next chapter?

Chapter Two: *If We All End Up Dying, What's the Purpose of Living?*

Recall what you wanted to be, and reflect on how that turned out; did you choose your purpose? Or did it choose you? Press the reset button and ask, *Why do I get up in the morning?*

Chapter Three: *Aren't I Somebody?*

Who is your aging exemplar, and why do you admire this person? What qualities of growing old does he or she embody? No need to try to be this person; learn from them and become the best version of you!

Chapter Four: *Am I Living the Good Life My Whole Life?*

Reimagine your vision of the good life. Are you living in the place you love with people you love, doing work you love on purpose? If so, how can you build on that? If not, how can you move toward that vision?

Chapter Five: *How Do I Stop Living a Default Life?*

What are your core values? We can accept certain values because we've been taught that they're important, but sometimes they just don't fit us anymore. What do you stand for? What won't you stand for? Who stands with you?

Chapter Six: *Am I Having a Late-Life Crisis?*

Select a committed listener who will listen to your answers to the "late-life crisis" questions in chapter 6. Explore ways to turn crisis into calling.

Chapter Seven: *Will I Earn a Passing Grade in Life?*

What do you want your legacy to be? How do you wish to be remembered by those whose lives you have touched? Create your own celebration of life, and share it with those you care about.

Chapter Eight: *How Can I Grow Whole as I Grow Old?*

Ask yourself, "How can I grow and give?" Review your calendar. Make regular appointments with yourself to grow and to give.

Chapter Nine: *How Will My Music Play On?*

Write a letter from the afterlife to your present life. What advice do you have for yourself today from the person who is able to look back on your entire life?

Acknowledgments

Though our names are the ones on the front cover, many people played important roles in creating this book. Heartfelt appreciation goes to our editor, Neal Maillet, who was, from day one, staunch in his support and enthusiasm. And, it's been a joy, once again, to work with Jeevan Sivasubramaniam, managing director, Editorial, and the entire Berrett-Koehler team.

A special call-out of appreciation to those who took the time to share their inspiring personal stories: Dan Buettner, Chip Conley, Chris Farrell, Tracy Hudson, Mary Jo Kreitzer, Parker Palmer, Ed Rapp, Tom Schreier, Deborah Szekely, Joel Theisen, Bill Thomas, and Cathy Wurzer. Without their wisdom and insights, this book would not exist.

Deepest appreciation goes to our spouses, Sally Humphries Leider and Jennifer Dixon, without whose patience and support this book would not have had the time and focus it needed.

Finally, with appreciation, we thank each other. This was a true collaboration. The result is a book that greatly exceeds what either of us could have done on our own.

Index

About the Authors

© REBECCA SLATER

Richard J. Leider

An internationally best-selling author and coach, Richard Leider is the founder of Inventure—The Purpose Company, whose mission is to help people "unlock the power of purpose" and answer the question "Why do you get up in the morning?" He is ranked by *Forbes* as one of the "Top 5" most respected coaches.

Richard has written or cowritten 11 books (six with Dave), including three best sellers, which have sold over one million copies. *Repacking Your Bags* and *The Power of Purpose* are considered classics in the personal growth field.

Widely viewed as a pioneer of the global purpose movement, Richard has had his work featured in many media sources, and his PBS Special, *The Power of Purpose*, was viewed by millions.

He has taken his purpose message to all 50 states, Canada, and four continents, and has advised a range of individuals and organizations, from AARP to the National Football League to the US State Department.

During his career, Richard has addressed more than two million people worldwide in his speeches to corporate, association, and social service groups. He lives on the St. Croix River in the Minneapolis area with his wife, Sally, an educator and life coach.

Dave Shapiro

Dave Shapiro is a philosopher, educator, and writer whose work consistently explores matters of meaning, purpose, and equity in the lives of young people and adults. He is a tenured philosophy professor at Cascadia College, a community college in the Seattle area, and is an adjunct lecturer in the Philosophy Department at the University of Washington, where he has a longstanding leadership role with the UW Center for Philosophy for Children.

Dave has coauthored five books with Richard Leider; he has also published two books of his own on ethics and philosophy with young people.

In 2018–2019, Dave was a Fulbright Academic and Professional Excellence Scholar; his project, "Cross-Pollinating Philosophy for Children in India and the US," took him to South India, where he worked with scholars and educators to bring philosophical inquiry into the lives of students at a number of schools in the states of Karnataka, Tamil Nadu, and Kerala.

Dave is a dedicated environmentalist and a full-time bicycle commuter; he lives in Seattle with his wife, the artist Jennifer Dixon.

Also by Richard J. Leider and David A. Shapiro

Repacking Your Bags
Lighten Your Load for the Good Life, Third Ed.

"Living in the place you belong, with the people you love, doing the right work, on purpose." In this wise and practical guide, Leider and Shapiro help you weigh all that you're carrying, leverage what helps you live well, and let go of those burdens that merely weigh you down.

Paperback, ISBN 978-1-60994-549-7
PDF ebook, ISBN 978-1-60994-552-7
ePub ebook, ISBN 978-1-60994-551-0

Claiming Your Place at the Fire
Living the Second Half of Your Life on Purpose

This book provides a new model for vital aging. It shows you how to age successfully by living on purpose. If you're in, or about to enter, "the second half of life," this practical guide will show you how to claim your rightful place among the "new elders."

Paperback, ISBN 978-1-57675-297-5
PDF ebook, ISBN 978-1-57675-877-9
ePub ebook, ISBN 978-1-60994-331-8

Berrett–Koehler Publishers, Inc.
www.bkconnection.com

800.929.2929

Also by Richard J. Leider

The Power of Purpose
Find Meaning, Live Longer, Better, Third Edition

Purpose is fundamental and gives life meaning. It gives us the will not just to live but to live long and well. In this new edition of his bestselling classic, legendary personal coach Richard Leider offers brand-new tools and techniques for unlocking it.

Paperback, ISBN 978-1-62656-636-1
PDF ebook, ISBN 978-1-62656-637-8
ePub ebook ISBN 978-1-62656-638-5
Digital audio, 978-1-62656-763-4

Life Reimagined
Discovering Your New Life Possibilities

Are you at a point in your life where you're asking, "What's next?" You've finished one chapter and you have yet to write the next one. Many of us face these transitions at midlife, but they can happen at any point. It's a time full of enormous potential, and it's called Life Reimagined.

Paperback, ISBN 978-1-60994-932-7
PDF ebook, ISBN 978-1-60994-953-2
ePub ebook ISBN 978-1-60994-954-9

Berrett–Koehler Publishers, Inc.
www.bkconnection.com   800.929.2929

Berrett–Koehler
Publishers

Berrett-Koehler is an independent publisher dedicated to an ambitious mission: *Connecting people and ideas to create a world that works for all.*

Our publications span many formats, including print, digital, audio, and video. We also offer online resources, training, and gatherings. And we will continue expanding our products and services to advance our mission.

We believe that the solutions to the world's problems will come from all of us, working at all levels: in our society, in our organizations, and in our own lives. Our publications and resources offer pathways to creating a more just, equitable, and sustainable society. They help people make their organizations more humane, democratic, diverse, and effective (and we don't think there's any contradiction there). And they guide people in creating positive change in their own lives and aligning their personal practices with their aspirations for a better world.

And we strive to practice what we preach through what we call "The BK Way." At the core of this approach is *stewardship,* a deep sense of responsibility to administer the company for the benefit of all of our stakeholder groups, including authors, customers, employees, investors, service providers, sales partners, and the communities and environment around us. Everything we do is built around stewardship and our other core values of *quality, partnership, inclusion,* and *sustainability.*

This is why Berrett-Koehler is the first book publishing company to be both a B Corporation (a rigorous certification) and a benefit corporation (a for-profit legal status), which together require us to adhere to the highest standards for corporate, social, and environmental performance. And it is why we have instituted many pioneering practices (which you can learn about at www.bkconnection.com), including the Berrett-Koehler Constitution, the Bill of Rights and Responsibilities for BK Authors, and our unique Author Days.

We are grateful to our readers, authors, and other friends who are supporting our mission. We ask you to share with us examples of how BK publications and resources are making a difference in your lives, organizations, and communities at www.bkconnection.com/impact.

Dear reader,

Thank you for picking up this book and welcome to the worldwide BK community! You're joining a special group of people who have come together to create positive change in their lives, organizations, and communities.

What's BK all about?

Our mission is to connect people and ideas to create a world that works for all.

Why? Our communities, organizations, and lives get bogged down by old paradigms of self-interest, exclusion, hierarchy, and privilege. But we believe that can change. That's why we seek the leading experts on these challenges—and share their actionable ideas with you.

A welcome gift

To help you get started, we'd like to offer you a free copy of one of our bestselling ebooks:

www.bkconnection.com/welcome

When you claim your **free ebook,** you'll also be subscribed to our blog.

Our freshest insights

Access the best new tools and ideas for leaders at all levels on our blog at ideas.bkconnection.com.

Sincerely,

Your friends at Berrett-Koehler